TANKS
OF WORLD WAR II

TANKS

OF WORLD WAR II

Steve Crawford

Grange
BOOKS

This edition published in 2000 by Grange Books
Grange Books plc
The Grange
1–6 Kingsnorth Estate
Hoo
Near Rochester
Kent ME3

Editorial and design:
Brown Partworks Limited
8 Chapel Place
Rivington Street
London
EC2A 3DQ
UK

Printed in Hong Kong

Editor: Chris Westhorp
Picture research: Antony Shaw
Design: Spencer Holbrook
Production: Matt Weyland

Picture Credits
All photographs The Robert Hunt Library except:
Tthe tank Museum, Bovington: 88

CONTENTS

VICKERS MEDIUM

SPECIFICATIONS

VICKERS MEDIUM TANK

Designation:
Vickers Medium Mk IIA

Secondary Armament:
4 x 7.5mm & 2 x .303in

Type:
Medium Tank

Engine:
Armstrong-Siddeley V-8

Length:
5.36m (17.6ft)

Range:
257km (160 miles)

Width:
2.77m (9.1ft)

Speed:
24km/h (15mph)

Height:
2.68m (8.8ft)

Fording:
.85m (2.78ft)

Weight:
13,440kg (29,568lb)

Trench Crossing:
1.75m (5.75ft)

Crew:
Five

Armour (hull):
8.25mm (.32in)

Main Armament:
3pdr QF

Armour (turret):
8.25mm (.32in)

In 1928, Australia purchased four Medium Mk IIA tanks from Great Britain. They differed from the British version by having the coaxial Vickers machine gun on the left of the 3-pounder gun, with a ball-mounted Vickers machine gun on the right. The Vickers Medium tanks were radical for their time, as they were the first tanks with a 360-degree traversing turret to be adopted by the British Army. It is indeed a sign of the rapid development of tank design in the 1930s that they were obsolete by 1939.

The design history of the Vickers is a mystery, as there are no records of correspondence pertaining to it, and no trials reports or memos. However, it was undoubtedly ordered and produced in haste in order to use funds allocated for a new tank by the British Treasury before the financial year ended (the first production models rolled off the factory line in 1923). As well as the fully traversing turret, the Vickers employed a sprung running gear. This was made possible by doing away with the overall track layout of the World War I heavy tanks, and thus lowering the top run of the track. The primary role of the Vickers was one of exploitation – hence its relatively high speed – rather than infantry support. Though obsolete by the outbreak of World War II, it was still used as a training tank.

CHAR B1

The Char B1 was the result of a request for a new French battle tank, and production began in 1935. Though the Char B will forever be associated with the disastrous 1940 campaign and the defeat of the French Army, the tank was in fact of an advanced design.

The specification for the Char B had its origin as far back as 1921, but delays and bureaucratic wrangling meant that the final design was not agreed until 1926. Nevertheless, the result was a good tank. It had self-sealing petrol tanks, a fireproof bulkhead, a gyroscopic compass, an electric starter, lubrication points connected by pipes to grouped lubricators, and a floor escape hatch that was also used for the disposal of empty cases. As steering was through a double differential combined with a hydrostatic unit in the steering drive, lining up the 75mm gun with a target was easy.

The tank ran on a Holt suspension improved by the firm FCM, and was fully covered by skirting. The B1's main problem was the poor distribution of the four-man crew, with the one-man turret being served by the commander, who also had to give orders to the crew, watch his own and enemy units, as well as load and fire the gun. In general with other French tanks, individual crew members felt isolated inside the B1. However, they were relatively well protected by the B1's armour.

SPECIFICATIONS

CHAR B1

Designation: **Char de Bataille B1**	*Secondary Armament:* **2 x 7.5mm**
Type: **Heavy Tank**	*Engine:* **Renault six-cylinder**
Length: **6.37m (20.92ft)**	*Range:* **180km (112 miles)**
Width: **2.5m (8.11ft)**	*Speed:* **27.5km/h (17.mph)**
Height: **2.8m (9.2ft)**	*Fording:* **Unknown**
Weight: **30,545kg (67,200lb)**	*Trench Crossing:* **2.74m (9ft)**
Crew: **Four**	*Armour (hull):* **14mm (.6in)**
Main Armament: **1 x 75mm, 1 x 47mm**	*Armour (turret):* **14mm (.6in)**

CHAR B1-BIS

SPECIFICATIONS

CHAR B1-BIS

Designation:
Char de Bataille B1-bis

Type:
Heavy Tank

Length:
6.38m (20.94ft)

Width:
2.5m (8.11ft)

Height:
2.79m (9.17ft)

Weight:
32,581m (71,680lb)

Crew:
Four

Main Armament:
1 x 75mm, 1 x 47mm

Secondary Armament:
2 x 7.5mm

Engine:
Renault six-cylinder

Range:
180km (112.5 miles)

Speed:
27.52km/h (17.2mph)

Fording:
Unknown

Trench Crossing:
2.74m (9ft)

Armour (hull):
14mm (.6in)

Armour (turret):
65mm (2.6in)

Based on the Char B1, the B1-bis had armour thickness increased to 65mm (2.6in) and was fitted with a new APX4 turret and gun. The first models were fitted with a 250hp engine, though this was later replaced by a 300hp aircraft motor. In addition, the later production models had a greater range thanks to auxiliary fuel tanks.

The bis was produced from 1937 by Renault, FAMH, Saint-Chamond and Schneider, with AMX also becoming involved in the manufacturing process in 1939. By the time of the German invasion of France in May 1940 some 380 Char Bs had been built, all of them bis models save for 35 of the earlier B1 variants.

The Char B was the main strike force of the four French armoured divisions in 1940, and as such represented the most significant Allied tank during the campaign (its 75mm gun could knock out any German tank then in service). Each division was composed of four battalions of tanks, made up of two battalions of Char B1-bis types and two battalions of light tanks. Those Char B1s that had not been destroyed in the fighting in France were used by the Germans as training vehicles, flamethrowers or for self-propelled mountings. In German service they performed well – testimony to the overall sound design of the vehicle.

CHAR S-35

The S-35 was regarded as the best tank in French service in 1940, and because of its excellent design the Germans pressed many into their own service after the fall of France in 1940. The S-35 had a similar turret design to the Char B1, but was faster with a road speed of 15.62km/h (25mph). Though the hull was rather high, its armour was well-shaped and rounded to deflect shots.

The 47mm main gun and coaxial 7.5mm machine gun were mounted in an electrically traversed turret which was probably better than anything the Germans possessed in 1940. That said, as ever, the turret performance was degraded by the fact that the commander was also the gunner. The tank was powered by a Somua V-8 190hp engine linked to a synchronised five-speed gearbox, which transmitted the drive to the tracks via rear sprockets.

The S-35 comprised one of the principal fighting vehicles of the French mechanised cavalry divisions, with each division having one regiment of S-35s. The tank ran over the nine road wheels each side, all protected by skirting plates. The first armoured fighting vehicle with an all-cast hull and turret construction, a total of 500 S-35s were built. At the time of the invasion of Poland in September 1939, the French Army had 261 S-35s; the rest were provided in response to increased production.

CHAR S-35

Designation: **Char de Cavalerie S-35**	*Secondary Armament:* **1 x 7.5mm**
Type: **Medium Tank**	*Engine:* **Somua V-8 190hp**
Length: **5.28m (17.33ft)**	*Range:* **257km (160.6 miles)**
Width: **1.85m (6.06ft)**	*Speed:* **15.62km/h (25mph)**
Height: **2.6m (8.58ft)**	*Fording:* **.8m (2.62ft)**
Weight: **20,363kg (44,800lb)**	*Trench Crossing:* **1.6m (5.25ft)**
Crew: **Three**	*Armour (hull):* **36mm (1.4in)**
Main Armament: **47mm**	*Armour (turret):* **55mm (2.16in)**

CHAR LEGER H-38

SPECIFICATIONS

CHAR LEGER H-38

Designation:
Char Léger Hotchkiss H-38

Type:
Light Tank

Length:
4.21m (13.83ft)

Width:
1.95m (6.39in)

Height:
2.13m (7ft)

Weight:
12,218kg (26,880lb)

Crew:
Two

Main Armament:
37mm

Secondary Armament:
1 x 7.5mm

Engine:
Hotchkiss six-cylinder

Range:
150km (93.75 miles)

Speed:
36km/h (22mph)

Fording:
.85m (2.78ft)

Trench Crossing:
1.8m (5.9ft)

Armour (hull):
34mm (1.3in)

Armour (turret):
45mm (1.77in)

Similar to the H-35, the Hotchkiss H-38 had a larger-capacity engine (5976cc) which developed 120hp at 2800rpm. In 1940 the French had 800 H-38s in service, and many were used by the German Army after the fall of France. Some turretless models were used by the artillery as tractors, others became ammunition carriers, and a few were modified to fire rockets to provide artillery support. Steering was controlled by means of a Cleveland differential, with the tracks being driven by front sprockets.

Essentially a cavalry tank, it was produced for the French Army from 1936 onwards. Its one-man APXR 1 turret housed a short-barrelled 37mm gun and a single machine gun. With one extra road wheel each side, the tank had a long track base which gave good cross-country performance at speed.

In German use, H-38s were issued to newly raised units and to units that were reforming in France after suffering heavy losses in Russia. Between 1941 and 1943, units equipped with H-38s were sent to Norway and the Balkans. On 30 December 1944, there were still 29 H-38s in German service. The H-39 variant was fitted with a new engine and a long-barrelled 37mm main gun. It was used by the Germans on the Eastern Front and Mediterranean, and also by Free French forces.

CHAR LEGER R-35

The R-35 was built by Renault as a replacement for its predecessor, the FT-17. A two-man vehicle, it was designed to re-equip the tank regiments supporting infantry divisions. As such it was reasonably well armoured and armed, though its Renault four-cylinder 82hp engine achieved a top speed of only 19.2km/h (12mph) – though this was deemed adequate for its roles of accompanying infantry.

The rear-mounted engine drove sprockets at the front of the track, with the suspension consisting of five road wheels and a low-mounted idler wheel at the rear on each side. The wheels themselves were mounted in two articulated bogies, each of two wheels, while wheel movement was controlled by springs made up of horizontally mounted rubber washers. The R-35 was an important element in the French rearmament programme in the 1930s, and it equipped 23 battalions by the time of the German invasion of France in 1940.

There was an improved model of the R-35 which was equipped with the longer-barrelled SA 38 37mm gun, while the R-40 variant was fitted with an entirely new suspension system designed by AMX, with armoured side skirts. This vehicle had far better cross-country performance that the R-35, but only two battalions had been equipped with it by 1940.

SPECIFICATIONS

CHAR LEGER R-35

Designation: **Char Léger Renault R-35**	*Secondary Armament:* **1 x 7.5mm**
Type: **Light Tank**	*Engine:* **Renault four-cylinder**
Length: **4m (13.16ft)**	*Range:* **140km (87.5 miles)**
Width: **1.85m (6.06ft)**	*Speed:* **19.2km/h (12mph)**
Height: **2.08m (6.83ft)**	*Fording:* **.8m (2.62ft)**
Weight: **10,181kg (22,400lb)**	*Trench Crossing:* **1.6m (5.25ft)**
Crew: **Two**	*Armour (hull):* **32mm (1.25in)**
Main Armament: **37mm**	*Armour (turret):* **45mm (1.77in)**

RENAULT FT

SPECIFICATIONS

RENAULT FT

Designation:
  Renault FT

Type:
  Light Tank

Length:
  4m (13.25ft)

Width:
  1.71m (5.61ft)

Height:
  2.13m (7ft)

Weight:
  6618kg (14,560lb)

Crew:
  Two

Main Armament:
  1 x 7.5mm/37mm gun

Secondary Armament:
  None

Engine:
  Renault four-cylinder

Range:
  35.4km (22 miles)

Speed:
  7.68km/h (4.8mph)

Fording:
  .9m (3ft)

Trench Crossing:
  1.8m (5.9ft)

Armour (hull):
  16mm (.63in)

Armour (turret):
  22mm (.86in)

The FT series of tanks was originally conceived as a light tank to accompany infantry units on the battlefield in World War I. The first time it was used in battle was on 31 May 1918 in the Forest of Retz. Suspension consisted of leaf springs combined with a vertical coil which tensioned the upper track run. Its front idlers were of the steel-rimmed laminated wood type.

During the 1930s the FT (on the right in the above photograph) series was still in service, though by this time the new 7.5mm Model 31 machine gun had superseded the 8mm Hotchkiss variant. The FT-17 variant of the tank was equipped with the 37mm Puteaux gun, with production of this model totalling 1830. In 1939 the French still had 1600 FTs in their army.

Both cannon- and machine gun-armed Renault FTs were supplied to Belgium, Brazil, Canada, China, Czechoslovakia, Finland, Holland, Japan, Poland, Spain and the United States. After the fall of France in June 1940, the Germans used many FT tanks for internal security duties. In addition, some FT turrets were incorporated as observation cupolas into the Atlantic Wall defences. A version which was armed with a short-barrelled 75mm gun was called the Renault BS. Only a few were built, but some were encountered in Axis service in North Africa by the Allies.

BRUMMBÄR

The Sturmpanzer IV (Brummbär) carried the 150mm StuH43 gun on a standard Panzer IV chassis. It was developed by Alkett, who designed the superstructure, while Krupp redesigned the Panzer IV chassis. Hitler, thinking they could be more potent than the StuG III, ordered the Brummbär into production at the end of 1942. Initial production began in April 1943, with a first batch of 60 being completed by May (this series had an armour plate 50mm [1.96in] thick bolted on to the basic 50mm- [1.96in-] thick hull front).

These vehicles had sliding-shutter visors for the driver, similar to those mounted on the Tiger I. However, in the later vehicles the driver was provided with a periscope. Full-scale production began in November 1943 and continued until the end of World War II. By that time 298 had been built. The final version of the vehicle had a redesigned superstructure which incorporated a ball-mounted machine gun in the top left-hand corner of the front plate, plus a cupola for the commander.

The first Brummbärs were issued to Sturmpanzer Abteilung 216 just prior to the Kursk Offensive in July 1943. A further three Sturmpanzer Abteilungs were raised (217, 218 and 219), and all of them saw service on the Eastern Front, as well as in the West and Italy.

SPECIFICATIONS

BRUMMBÄR

Designation: **StuG IV 15cm StuH43**	Secondary Armament: **2 x 7.92mm**
Type: **Assault Infantry Gun**	Engine: **Maybach HL120TRM**
Length: **5.93m (19.45ft)**	Range: **210km (131 miles)**
Width: **2.88m (9.44ft)**	Speed: **40km/h (28.12mph)**
Height: **2.52m (8.26ft)**	Fording: **1m (3.25ft)**
Weight: **28,712kg (63,168lb)**	Trench Crossing: **2.2m (7.25ft)**
Crew: **Five**	Armour (hull): **80mm (3.14in)**
Main Armament: **150mm**	Armour (turret): **100mm (3.93in)**

GRILLE

SPECIFICATIONS

GRILLE

Designation:
SdKfz 138/1

Secondary Armament:
1 x 7.92mm

Type:
SP Heavy Infantry Gun

Engine:
Praga EPA/2

Length:
4.61m (14ft)

Range:
185km (115.6 miles)

Width:
2.16m (7.08ft)

Speed:
35km/h (21.87mph)

Height:
2.4m (7.87ft)

Fording:
.9m (3ft)

Weight:
11,709kg (25,760lb)

Trench Crossing:
1.87m (6.13ft)

Crew:
Five

Armour (hull):
50mm (1.96in)

Main Armament:
150mm

Armour (turret):
25mm (.98in)

The Grille was first ordered for construction on the new self-propelled gun chassis that BMM was developing, the resultant vehicle being designated Sf 38(t) Ausf K. However, wartime demands resulted in Panzer 38(t)s being used instead, being converted by BMM as they returned from the front for refits. The standard chassis was fitted with a new fighting compartment superstructure, which had to be extended over the engine compartment in order to accommodate the sIG33/1 L/12 heavy gun and its 15 rounds of ammunition.

A total of 90 were produced between February and April 1943. All Grilles were issued to the heavy infantry assault gun companies of panzergrenadier regiments, serving in Russia, Tunisia, Italy and France from early 1943. In June 1944, at the time of the D-Day landings, the Grille was still in service with the 38th Panzer Heavy Infantry Assault Gun Abteilung of the 2nd Panzer Division in Normandy.

The Praga EPA/2 engine had five forward gears and one reverse, and gave a top speed of 35km/h (21.87mph). As with most infantry assault guns, the crew were housed in an open superstructure, though the provision of an MG34 machine gun gave them some protection from enemy infantry antitank squads.

HUMMEL

The Hummel was an attempt to provide armoured units with artillery support on a fully tracked armoured chassis. The 150mm sFH18/1L/30 gun was mounted on a Panzer IV chassis, though this was only intended as an interim measure until a chassis designed specifically for self-propelled gun platforms could be developed and produced. To accommodate the gun, the engine was moved forward to a central position, while the Hummel's drive sprocket was of the type designed for the Panzer III. The open-topped fighting compartment was enclosed on all four sides by slanted armour plates bolted to the hull, while the glacis plate was extended and there was a small compartment for the driver on the left-hand side.

The gun was mounted over the engine, which gave the Hummel a high silhouette. The specially designed ammunition carriers acted as supply vehicles for the Hummels, and 157 were built in total.

The Hummel was issued to the panzer divisions, where they served in the heavy batteries of the armoured artillery detachments. At first each panzer division was equipped with six Hummels in a single heavy battery, though later a second heavy battery was added. They fought at Kursk in mid-1943, and continued in service until the end of the war in May 1945.

SPECIFICATIONS

HUMMEL

Designation: SdKfz 165	**Secondary Armament:** 1 x 7.92mm
Type: SP Heavy Howitzer	**Engine:** HL 120TRM
Length: 7.17m (23.52ft)	**Range:** 215km (134.4 miles)
Width: 2.87m (9.41ft)	**Speed:** 42km/h (26.25mph)
Height: 2.81m (9.23ft)	**Fording:** .99m (3.25ft)
Weight: 24,436kg (53,760lb)	**Trench Crossing:** 2.2m (7.25ft)
Crew: Five	**Armour (hull):** 30mm (1.18in)
Main Armament: 150mm	**Armour (turret):** 10mm (.39in)

JAGDPANTHER

SPECIFICATIONS

JAGDPANTHER

Designation: **SdKfz 173**	Secondary Armament: **1 x 7.92mm**
Type: **Heavy Tank Destroyer**	Engine: **Maybach HL230P30**
Length: **9.9m (32.8ft)**	Range: **160km (100 miles)**
Width: **3.27m (10.72ft)**	Speed: **46km/h (28.75mph)**
Height: **2.72m (8.92ft)**	Fording: **1.7m (5.57ft)**
Weight: **46,836kg (103,040lb)**	Trench Crossing: **1.9m (6.23ft)**
Crew: **Five**	Armour (hull): **60mm (2.36in)**
Main Armament: **88mm**	Armour (turret): **80mm (3.14in)**

An order to develop a heavy assault gun by mating the 88mm Pak L/71 gun to a Panther chassis was given on 2 October 1942, and a wooden mock-up was completed by October 1943. Hitler saw the prototype on 16 December 1943, and production began in January 1944.

The upper hull plates and side plates of the standard Panther chassis were extended to create the fighting compartment. The 88mm Pak 43/3 gun was installed in a gun mount in the sloping front plate (early production vehicles had the gun mount welded to the superstructure front plate). Later production models had a gun mount which was protruded and was bolted in place. Defence against enemy infantry was provided by a *Hahverteidigungsgerät* (close-defence weapon) mounted in the superstructure roof, plus a machine gun in a hull mount in the superstructure front.

The Jagdpanther was one of the finest tank destroyers of the war. The first vehicles were issued to the 559th and 654th Anti-Tank Battalions, though only the 654th received the full complement of 42 vehicles. The largest assembly of Jagdpanthers in the war took place during the Ardennes Offensive in December 1944. Thereafter they were also issued to the tank detachments of at least seven panzer divisions. In total, 392 were produced between January 1944 and March 1945.

MARDER II

The Marder II antitank vehicle was essentially a 75mm Pak 40/2 gun mated to a Panzer II chassis. By May 1942 the combat effectiveness of the Panzer II (still being produced at a rate of 50 per month) was being questioned – it was certainly obsolete by this date. As a result, early in June it was decided that half the production would be given to mounting the Pak 40 gun on the Panzer II chassis, though assembly was cut short in June 1943 to concentrate on production of the Wespe (see page 42).

The hull and superstructure front of the Marder II remained the same as the standard Panzer II Ausf F. A further superstructure was built to create the fighting compartment, with the upper half of the field-carriage mount for the Pak 40 being retained. However, girders were added to provide support for the gun. Secondary armament for the three-man crew was provided by one 7.92mm MG 34 machine gun, while 37 rounds were carried for the main gun.

A total of 576 Marder IIs were built between June 1942 and June 1943, with a further 75 Panzer IIs being converted between July 1943 and March 1944. The vehicles were issued to antitank detachments from July 1942 onwards, and served in both the East and West until the end of the war.

SPECIFICATIONS

MARDER II

Designation:
SdKfz 131

Type:
SP Antitank Gun

Length:
6.36m (20.86ft)

Width:
2.28m (7.48ft)

Height:
2.2m (7.21ft)

Weight:
10,996kg (24,192lb)

Crew:
Three

Main Armament:
75mm

Secondary Armament:
1 x 7.92mm

Engine:
Maybach HL62TRM

Range:
190km (118.7 miles)

Speed:
40km/h (25mph)

Fording:
.85m (2.78ft)

Trench Crossing:
1.75m (5.74ft)

Armour (hull):
35mm (1.37in)

Armour (superstructure):
30mm (1.18in)

MARDER III

SPECIFICATIONS

MARDER III

Designation:
SdKfz 138

Type:
SP Antitank Gun

Length:
4.95m (16.24ft)

Width:
2.15m (7.05ft)

Height:
2.48m (8.13ft)

Weight:
10,691kg (23,520lb)

Crew:
Four

Main Armament:
75mm

Secondary Armament:
1 x 7.92mm

Engine:
Praga AC

Range:
190km (118.75 miles)

Speed:
42km/h (26.25mph)

Fording:
.9m (3ft)

Trench Crossing:
1.87m (6.13ft)

Armour (hull):
20mm (.78in)

Armour (superstructure):
10mm (.39in)

On orders from Hitler, in July 1942 production capacity of the Panzer 38(t) was switched to self-propelled gun chassis. This prompted a new design in which the engine was moved to the centre of the vehicle, which allowed the gun to be moved to the rear. In addition, frontal armour was reduced, which also lessened overall weight.

The vehicle mounted the the potent 75mm Pak 40/3 gun, and at the beginning of February 1943 Hitler was informed that production would reach 150 units per month (though this level was not reached until November of that year). In May 1944, production of the Marder III was terminated in favour of the Jagdpanzer Hetzer. By that time a total of 975 vehicles had been produced for the army.

Those Marders built during 1943 had a rounded, cast cover for the driving compartment at the front right-hand side of the vehicle. At the end of 1943, a simpler welded cover was introduced, with the front towing tugs formed from extensions of the side armour plate.

The Marder III was deployed to the antitank detachments of both panzer and infantry divisions from May 1943. They served on all fronts during the war, especially on the Eastern Front, and at the end of the war there were still over 300 in Wehrmacht service.

NASHORN

The Nashorn (Rhinoceros), later called Hornisse (Hornet), was designed to accommodate the 88mm Pak 43/1 L/71 gun – the most powerful tank armament produced by the Germans in World War II, and the most effective anti-armour gun built by either side. With a muzzle velocity of 1018m/sec (3340ft/sec), it could destroy any Allied tank in service up to the end of the war in Europe in May 1945.

In October 1942, it was decided to use 100 vehicles for the summer offensive on the Eastern Front from the initial order of 500. As with the Hummel (see page 15), the chassis used a lengthened Panzer IV hull with the motor moved forward to a central position.

Some 494 Nashorns were delivered between February 1943 and March 1945, and they were assigned to heavy antitank units which acted as independent formations attached to corps or armies. As such, they became highly effective mobile tank-hunting squads, especially on the Eastern Front, where they knocked out hundreds of Soviet T-34s. The first Wehrmacht unit to be equipped with Nashorns was the 655th Heavy Anti-Tank Battalion (schwere Panzerjägerabteilung) on the Eastern Front in the summer of 1943. In total, five other heavy tank-hunter units were formed, seeing service in Italy, the West and Russia.

SPECIFICATIONS

NASHORN

Designation: **SdKfz 164**	Secondary Armament: **1 x 7.92mm**
Type: **SP Heavy Antitank Gun**	Engine: **Maybach HL120TRM**
Length: **8.44m (27.69ft)**	Range: **190km (118.7 miles)**
Width: **2.86m (9.38ft)**	Speed: **215km (134.37 miles)**
Height: **2.65m (8.69ft)**	Fording: **.8m (2.62ft)**
Weight: **24,436kg (53,760lb)**	Trench Crossing: **2.3m (7.54ft)**
Crew: **Four**	Armour (hull): **30mm (1.18in)**
Main Armament: **88mm**	Armour (superstructure): **10mm (.39in)**

PAK 40 (SF)

SPECIFICATIONS

PAK 40 (SF)

Designation:
Geschützwagen 39H(f)

Type:
SP Antitank Gun

Length:
5.31m (17.42ft)

Width:
1.83m (6ft)

Height:
2.23m (7.31ft)

Weight:
8644kg (19,017lb)

Crew:
Four

Main Armament:
75mm

Secondary Armament:
1 x 7.92mm

Engine:
Hotchkiss Six-cylinder

Range:
150km (93.75 miles)

Speed:
36km/h (22.5mph)

Fording:
.8m (2.62ft)

Trench Crossing:
1.6m (5.25ft)

Armour (hull):
30mm (1.18in)

Armour (superstructure):
30mm (1.18in)

With the capture of so many vehicles following the fall of France in June 1940, the Germans set about converting them for their own use. This was not an immediate decision, as the army was flushed with victory and few believed that large numbers of non-German armoured fighting vehicles would be needed. It was only with the huge losses experienced on the Eastern Front, plus the appearance of the Soviet T-34, that prompted the necessity for large numbers of antitank platforms. One such vehicle was the PaK40 (SF), a self-propelled antitank gun on a light tank chassis. The conversion was unusual in that the engine was left in the rear.

The superstructure and engine cover were removed and a new plate for the driver was fitted as part of the new self-propelled gun conversion. The numbers converted were not great: a total of 24 were modified to carry the 75mm gun (this model is shown in the above photograph), while a further 48 were modified to mount the larger 105mm gun. In both models the gun had a traverse of 30 degrees to the left and right, with an elevation of plus 22 degrees to minus five degrees.

These self-propelled armoured fighting vehicles were assigned to the 8th Panzerartillerie Abteilung serving in France, and they saw action following the Allied D-Day landings in June 1944.

PANZER I

In the early 1930s the German Army needed a tank that could be built cheaply and in large numbers for training purposes. The Krupp design (the L.K.A.1) was selected as the first production model in 1934, eventually becoming the Panzer IA. The earliest versions had open-top hulls, no turrets and were designated as agricultural tractors to disguise their true purpose.

The layout comprised a rear-mounted engine with the transmission led forward to front-driving sprockets. The crew compartment was in the centre of the vehicle, with the driver on the left. The turret, armed with two machine guns, was off-set to the right on the roof of the hull. Suspension consisted of independently sprung front road wheels with the remaining wheels in pairs on leaf springs linked by a girder for extra rigidity.

Production of the Panzer IA ran to 500 vehicles, with nearly 2000 of the B variant being produced. In 1936 both types were battle-tested during the Spanish Civil War. It was soon discovered that the absence of an antitank gun and the two-man turret were major disadvantages. By 1939, insufficient numbers of the more powerful Panzer II and Panzer III had been built, and so the Panzer I saw service in Poland in 1939 and France in 1940. Despite its obsolescence, a few Panzer Is saw service during the invasion of Russia in 1941.

SPECIFICATIONS

PANZER I

Designation: Sdkfz 101	**Secondary Armament:** None
Type: Light Tank	**Engine:** Krupp M305
Length: 4.02m (13.18ft)	**Range:** 145km (90.62 miles)
Width: 2.06m (6.75ft)	**Speed:** 37km/h (23.12mph)
Height: 1.72m (5.64ft)	**Fording:** .85m (2.78ft)
Weight: 5498kg (12,096lb)	**Trench Crossing:** 1.75m (5.74ft)
Crew: Two	**Armour (hull):** 13mm (.51in)
Main Armament: 2 x 7.92mm	**Armour (turret):** 13mm (.51in)

PANZER II

SPECIFICATIONS

PANZER II

Designation:
SdKfz 121

Type:
Light Tank

Length:
4.81m (15.78ft)

Width:
2.3m (7.5ft)

Height:
1.99m (6.52ft)

Weight:
9061kg (19,936lb)

Crew:
Three

Main Armament:
20mm

Secondary Armament:
1 x 7.92mm

Engine:
Maybach HL62TR

Range:
200km (125 miles)

Speed:
40km/h (25mph)

Fording:
.85m (2.78ft)

Trench Crossing:
1.75m (5.74ft)

Armour (hull):
14.5mm (.57in)

Armour (turret):
14.5mm (.57in)

Designed by the company MAN, the Panzer II fulfilled a light tank requirement for the German Army. The first 25 pre-production machines were built in 1935, the basic design having a rear engine and front drive. During the initial stages the tank underwent a number of minor changes, such as turret modifications and work on the front superstructure. The main production versions were the Ausf B and C models, which had an angled nose, and splash plates on the top and bottom of the mantlet.

The Ausf D and E models were produced by Daimler-Benz in 1939, and incorporated a Famo/Christie-type suspension to give a top speed of 56km/h (35mph). However, cross-country performance was poor and these particular models were withdrawn from service early. The Ausf F, G and J models were improved versions of the Ausf C, which were up-armoured to give protection from heavier antitank guns. This meant 35mm (1.37in) of frontal armour and 20mm (.78in) of side armour.

The Ausf A–C models were widely used in the early period of World War II, especially in Poland in 1939 and France in 1940. At the beginning of the attack in the West in May 1940, for example, there were 965 Panzer IIs in German service – forming the backbone of the 2500 German tanks used in the campaign.

PANZER III AUSF F

During the 1930s, it was envisaged that the core of the German panzer divisions would be a medium tank armed with a 37mm or 50mm armour-piercing gun. A number of prototype vehicles were built by Daimler-Benz, Rheinmetall, MAN and Krupp in response to this requirement. Tested in 1936–37, the Daimler-Benz model was chosen for further development.

The early models – Ausf A, B, C and D – had different forms of suspension, ranging from five large road wheels on coil springs per side (on the Ausf A) to eight small wheels on leaf springs (on the Ausf B, C and D). The turret and hull were essentially the same in all models. In the Ausf E version the suspension consisted of six road wheels each side on a transverse torsion-bar system, and this arrangement would continue through the rest of the Panzer III's production life.

The Ausf F was similar to the Ausf E, the main difference being to the ignition system, with cast air intakes being added to the upper hull plate to allow air circulation for brakes and final-drive cooling. Most were armed with the 37mm KwK L/46.5 gun, but around 100 were equipped with the 50mm KwK L42 model. Between August 1940 and 1942, many of the those remaining were up-gunned to 50mm calibre, with more armour also being added to the hull and superstructure.

SPECIFICATIONS

PANZER III AUSF F

Designation: **SdKfz 141**	Secondary Armament: **2 x 7.92mm**
Type: **Medium Tank**	Engine: **Maybach HL120TRM**
Length: **5.38m (17.65ft)**	Range: **165km (101 miles)**
Width: **2.95m (9.67ft)**	Speed: **40km/h (25mph)**
Height: **2.44m (8ft)**	Fording: **.8m (2.62ft)**
Weight: **20,160kg (44,352lb)**	Trench Crossing: **2.59m (8.5ft)**
Crew: **Five**	Armour (hull): **30mm (1.18in)**
Main Armament: **37mm**	Armour (turret): **30mm (1.18in)**

PANZER III AUSF J

SPECIFICATIONS

PANZER III AUSF J

Designation: **SdKfz 141**	**Secondary Armament:** **2 x 7.92mm**
Type: **Medium Tank**	**Engine:** **Maybach HL120TRM**
Length: **5.52m (18.11ft)**	**Range:** **155km (96.8 miles)**
Width: **2.95m (9.67ft)**	**Speed:** **40km/h (25mph)**
Height: **2.5m (8.2ft)**	**Fording:** **.8m (2.62ft)**
Weight: **21,890kg (48,160lb)**	**Trench Crossing:** **2.59m (8.5ft)**
Crew: **Five**	**Armour (hull):** **30mm (1.18in)**
Main Armament: **50mm**	**Armour (turret):** **50mm (1.96in)**

The Panzer III Ausf J was the first variant of the tank to be built to have the armour protection increased to a basic 50mm (1.96in). The armour change required new fittings. In addition, an improved driver's visor was fitted, plus a new ball-shaped hull machine-gun mount. The upper hull front accommodated newly designed air intakes for brakes and final-drive cooling, while single-piece access hatches in the glacis were fitted in place of the double hatch.

The initial order for the Ausf J was for 900, but this was later increased to 2700. The new vehicle, with its 50mm KwK L/42 gun, was used to equip the 2nd and 5th Panzer Divisions, plus an independent panzer regiment. These units were sent to the Eastern Front in September 1941, where they took part in the later stages of Operation Barbarossa, the German invasion of the Soviet Union, suffering many losses (their engines and suspension systems suffered in the freezing conditions).

The rest of the Ausf Js were used as replacement vehicles for the 1400 Panzers II tanks lost during the first year of fighting in Russia and North Africa. Though the Panzer III was outclassed by the T-34 in the East from the end of 1941, there were still 500 KwK L/42-armed Panzer IIIs in service at the beginning of the German summer offensive in mid-1943.

PANZER III AUSF N

The Panzer III Ausf N was an attempt to increase the potency of the tank by arming it with the 75mm KwK L/24 gun. This weapon fired an effective high-explosive round and an excellent shaped-charge that had better penetration than the long-barrelled KwK39 L/60 which it replaced.

The initial order was for 450 tanks, but the troops at the front liked the Ausf N so much that Ausf M models were also equipped with the short-barrelled 75mm gun. With additional Panzer IIIs being so armed, the total number of Ausf Ns was brought up to 700.

The Ausf N was recognisable by its short-barrelled gun and the lack of spaced armour on the mantlet. Many of the later Ausf Ns were fitted with a new cupola with thicker armour and a single hatch in place of the earlier split-hatch design. Ausf Ns were also given side skirts for greater protection from March 1943.

In the field the Ausf N was used to provide close support for the Tigers (each heavy tank company had 10 Ausf Ns to nine Tigers), as the smaller vehicle was more agile at close quarters, whereas the Tiger was rather slow and vulnerable. The Ausf N was also used in the panzer regiments of the panzer divisions. In mid-1943, during the Kursk Offensive, German panzer units were equipped with 155 Panzer III Ausf Ns.

SPECIFICATIONS

PANZER III AUSF N

Designation: **SdKfz 141/2**	Secondary Armament: **2 x 7.92mm**
Type: **Medium Tank**	Engine: **Maybach HL120TRM**
Length: **5.65m (18.53ft)**	Range: **155km (96.8 miles)**
Width: **2.95m (9.67ft)**	Speed: **40km/h (25mph)**
Height: **2.5m (8.2ft)**	Fording: **.8m (2.62ft)**
Weight: **23,418kg (51,520lb)**	Trench Crossing: **2.59m (8.5ft)**
Crew: **Five**	Armour (hull): **50mm (1.96in)**
Main Armament: **75mm**	Armour (turret): **50mm (1.96in)**

PANZER IV AUSF C

SPECIFICATIONS

PANZER IV AUSF C

Designation:
SdKfz 161

Type:
Medium Support Tank

Length:
5.92m (19.42ft)

Width:
3.29m (10.79ft)

Height:
2.68m (8.79ft)

Weight:
19,345kg (42,560lb)

Crew:
Five

Main Armament:
75mm

Secondary Armament:
1 x 7.92mm

Engine:
Maybach HL120TRM

Range:
200km (125 miles)

Speed:
40km/h (25mph)

Fording:
1m (3.25ft)

Trench Crossing:
2.2m (7.25ft)

Armour (hull):
30mm (1.18in)

Armour (turret):
30mm (1.18in)

By far the most enduring of the main types of German tank, the Panzer IV was specified as a medium tank in the 20-ton class, to be armed with a 75mm gun. The order to build the vehicle was awarded to Krupp, who initially proposed interleaved road wheels for suspension. However, the actual suspension used was much more simple: eight road wheels on each side suspended in pairs on leaf springs. Like other German tanks of the period, the Panzer IV's engine was located at the rear with the transmission led forward to the final drive via sprockets at the front of the track.

The Ausf C, which was armed with the KwK 37 1/24 gun, incorporated a number of minor changes to the design of the Ausf B, including improved turret face, a new gun mantlet housing, an altered motor mount, and an armoured sleeve that protected the coaxial machine gun. Later, to extend combat life, additional armour plates were bolted to the hull and superstructure sides.

An initial order for the Ausf C was for 300 vehicles, but only 134 were completed. Production took place between September 1938 and August 1939, and the Ausf C saw service in Poland in 1939 and the West in the summer of 1940. The vehicle remained in service until 1943, but by then numbers had dwindled drastically due to battlefield attrition.

PANZER IV AUSF H

Between April 1943 and July 1944, a total of 3774 Panzer IV Ausf Hs were produced. The basic difference between this model and the Ausf G variant was the fitting of the SSG77 transmission. In addition, armour thickness was increased to 80mm (3.14in) from 50mm (1.96in). A host of other minor modifications included external air filters, all-steel rollers, a cupola mount for an antiaircraft machine gun, a new idler, the deletion of side vision ports for the driver and radio operator, and a new cupola with thicker armour.

Main armament consisted of the 75mm KwK40 L/48 gun. The Ausf H and J models were up-gunned with this weapon in 1943–44. It was an excellent all-round gun, which fired a potent high-explosive round and also had a good anti-armour performance. This was especially true at short ranges when using the PzGr40 armour-piercing, composite non-rigid round.

Following the introduction into service of the Panther, all panzer regiments in a panzer division were to have one detachment of Panthers and one detachment of Panzer IVs. However, because of problems with the Panther, panzer divisions had a second detachment of Panzer IVs. In France in June 1944, for example, most of the 748 Panzer IVs with the nine German panzer divisions were Ausf H models.

SPECIFICATIONS

PANZER IV AUSF H

Designation:
SdKfz 161/2

Type:
Medium Tank

Length:
7.02m (23.03ft)

Width:
3.29m (10.79ft)

Height:
2.68m (8.79ft)

Weight:
25,454kg (56,000lb)

Crew:
Five

Main Armament:
75mm

Secondary Armament:
1 x 7.92mm

Engine:
Maybach HL120TRM

Range:
210km (131 miles)

Speed:
38km/h (23.75mph)

Fording:
1m (3.25ft)

Trench Crossing:
2.2m (7.25ft)

Armour (hull):
80mm (3.14in)

Armour (turret):
50mm (1.96in)

PANZER V AUSF D

SPECIFICATIONS

PANZER V AUSF D

Designation: **SdKfz 171**	Secondary Armament: **2 x 7.92mm**
Type: **Heavy Medium Tank**	Engine: **Maybach HL 230P30**
Length: **8.86m (29.06ft)**	Range: **200km (125 miles)**
Width: **3.43m (11.25ft)**	Speed: **46km/h (28.75 miles)**
Height: **2.95m (9.67ft)**	Fording: **1.7m (5.57ft)**
Weight: **43,781kg (96,320lb)**	Trench Crossing: **1.91m (6.26ft)**
Crew: **Five**	Armour (hull): **80mm (3.14in)**
Main Armament: **75mm**	Armour (turret): **100mm (3.93in)**

After the shock of encountering the T-34 in late 1941, Hitler ordered the development of a similar tank in the 30-ton class. He ordered the MAN design into production on 14 May 1942, with factory lines beginning work in December. The Führer demanded that 250 be ready for his summer 1943 offensive on the Russian Front.

Though the Panther's combat debut at Kursk in mid-1943 was a failure, with many vehicles breaking down before they got into action, once the teething problems had been ironed out it became one of the finest tanks of the war. Very fast and manoeuvrable, the Panther incorporated interleaved road wheels with torsion-bar suspension, well-sloped hull and turret, a rear engine and front drive. The long 75mm KwK42 L/70 gun was mounted in an external, curved gun mantlet with an accompanying coaxial machine gun. The turret sides and rear also featured pistol ports.

The Ausf D entered production in January 1943, with the first vehicles being allocated to units in February. In April 1943, however, deliveries stopped and all vehicles were recalled for major modifications. Then, in May, the 51st and 52nd Tank Battalions received Panthers (mostly Ausf D) and saw action at the Battle of Kursk in July 1943. The 23rd and 26th Independent Panzer Regiments received Ausf Ds, as did the élite Waffen-SS divisions.

PANZER V AUSF G

As a result of recommendations and comments from troops in the field using the Panther Ausf A and D, the Ausf G incorporated a number of design changes. Chief among them was a redesigned hull, which incorporated increased side armour on the upper-hull side and a single-piece side plate. The driver's vision port was done away with, being replaced by a rotating periscope. In addition, the driver could drive with his head out of the hatch thanks to an adjustable seat and extendible controls.

Suspension was as standard, though in September 1944 a number of vehicles were fitted with steel-rimmed "silent bloc" wheels that became standard on the Ausf F in 1945. Other modifications included armoured ammunition bins, a heater system that drew warm air from a device over the left-side engine fan, and flame-trap exhaust mufflers.

The Ausf G saw service on the Eastern Front and in the West from March 1944 to the end of the war, during which time 3126 were produced. It comprised over half the tank strength of the panzer divisions in 1945, its KwK42 L/70 gun taking a heavy toll of Soviet tanks in the fighting in East Prussia and Hungary. However, by that late stage of the war the Panthers were unable to stop the deluge of Red Army armoured units.

SPECIFICATIONS

PANZER V AUSF G

Designation: **SdKfz 171**	*Secondary Armament:* **2 x 7.92mm**
Type: **Heavy Medium Tank**	*Engine:* **Maybach HL230P30**
Length: **8.86m (29.06ft)**	*Range:* **200km (125 miles)**
Width: **3.43m (11.25ft)**	*Speed:* **46km/h (28.75mph)**
Height: **2.98m (9.77ft)**	*Fording:* **1.7m (5.57ft)**
Weight: **46,327kg (101,920lb)**	*Trench Crossing:* **1.91m (6.26ft)**
Crew: **Five**	*Armour (hull):* **80mm (3.14in)**
Main Armament: **75mm**	*Armour (turret):* **110mm (4.33in)**

PANZER 35(T)

SPECIFICATIONS

PANZER 35(T)

Designation: **Panzerkampfwagen 35(t)**	Secondary Armament: **2 x 7.92mm**
Type: **Light Tank**	Engine: **Skoda T11**
Length: **4.9m (16.07ft)**	Range: **190km (119 miles)**
Width: **2.1m (6.88ft)**	Speed: **35km/h (21.87mph)**
Height: **2.35m (7.7ft)**	Fording: **1m (3.25ft)**
Weight: **10,690kg (23,520lb)**	Trench Crossing: **1.9m (6.23ft)**
Crew: **Four**	Armour (hull): **25mm (.98in)**
Main Armament: **37mm**	Armour (turret): **25mm (.98in)**

The Panzer 35(t) was a Czech-designed tank in the 10-ton class. As well as being rugged, much thought had gone into ease of operation. Thus, a 12-speed gearbox combined with a a pneumatic-servo-mechanical steering unit to make the tank easy to drive. In addition, the suspension system, consisting of two sets of four-wheel bogie units each side, was very hard wearing.

The four-man crew sat in a single compartment, with the engine at the rear. The tank's armament, like most Czech tanks of the period, consisted of a 37mm gun (in this case the Skoda A3) plus a coaxial 7.92mm machine gun and a second machine gun in the hull front.

Approximately 160 were built for the Czech Army, having the designation LT-35. Following the annexation of Czechoslovakia by Germany, 106 of these vehicles were given to the 6th Panzer Division. During the campaign in the West in 1940, the Panzer 35(t) formed the backbone of the armoured strength of this particular unit.

Though it performed well in Poland and the West in 1939–40, the 35(t)'s shortcomings became clear in Russia. When the 6th Panzer Division fought on the Eastern Front in 1941, for example, it lost half its Panzer 35(t)s in the first six months of combat. As well as the German Army, the Panzer 35(t) was used by the armed forces of Bulgaria, Romania and Slovakia.

PANZER 38(T)

The Czech LT-38 was one of the most successful products of the pre-war Czech armaments industry. Originating as a design in 1933, it was gradually improved so that by 1938 the latest version, the TNHP, was ordered for the Czech Army. Some 150 were ordered for the Czechs, while foreign orders totalled 200.

When the Germans took over the country in March 1939, they were pleased to have the tank and continued its production as the Panzer 38(t). They were soon issued to the 7th and 8th Panzer Divisions, and by 1941 this vehicle formed nearly 25 percent of the total Wehrmacht tank strength.

The centrally placed turret, mounted on the roof of the fighting compartment, carried the Skoda 37mm A7 gun and a 7.92mm machine gun, while another machine gun was mounted in the front of the hull on the left-hand side. Rugged, reliable and easy to maintain, the Germans were happy to keep building the Panzer 38(t) until 1942, by which time a total of 1168 had been produced. By this date it was obsolete as a frontline tank, but the chassis continued to be used as a platform for self-propelled guns. Before the Germans seized Czechoslovakia, the vehicle was sold abroad or built under licence. In some countries it continued in service into the late 1940s.

SPECIFICATIONS

PANZER 38(T)

Designation: Panzerkampfwagen 38(t)	**Secondary Armament:** 2 x 7.92mm
Type: Light Tank	**Engine:** Praga EPA
Length: 4.61m (15.12ft)	**Range:** 250km (156 miles)
Width: 2.13m (7ft)	**Speed:** 42km/h (26.25mph)
Height: 2.4m (7.87ft)	**Fording:** .9m (3ft)
Weight: 9672kg (21,280lb)	**Trench Crossing:** 1.87m (6.13ft)
Crew: Four	**Armour (hull):** 25mm (.98in)
Main Armament: 37mm	**Armour (turret):** 25mm (.98in)

PANZERJÄGER

SPECIFICATIONS

PANZERJÄGER

Designation:
Panzerjäger

Type:
SP Antitank Gun

Length:
4.42m (14.5ft)

Width:
2.06m (6.75ft)

Height:
2.25m (7.38ft)

Weight:
6516kg (14,336lb)

Crew:
Three

Main Armament:
47mm

Secondary Armament:
None

Engine:
Maybach NL38TR

Range:
140km (87 miles)

Speed:
40km/h (25mph)

Fording:
.85m (2.78ft)

Trench Crossing:
1.75m (5.74ft)

Armour (hull):
13mm (.51in)

Armour (superstructure):
13mm (.51in)

This vehicle was the first of Germany's "tank hunters", and consisted of a Czech 47mm antitank gun on a Panzer I Ausf B chassis (which by early 1940 was obsolete as a frontline tank). Some 170 tank chassis were converted by Alkett of Berlin-Spandau between March 1940 and February 1941.

The conversion was relatively simple, and involved nothing more than removing the tank turret and placing the gun and a three-sided shield in its place. The superstructure was open at the rear, and there was enough room inside for 86 rounds for the 47mm Pak(t) L43.4 gun. The latter was mounted within the shield on a pivoting mount supported by girders. The Maybach engine was driven by a gearbox that had five forward gears and one reverse.

The Panzerjäger was issued to five army antitank battalions, and it first saw action in Belgium and France in May and June 1940 during the German attack in the West. It proved adequate enough, though even at this early date it was becoming obsolete as a frontline fighting vehicle. In North Africa the vehicles saw service with the Afrika Korps in infantry antitank units, while it was also used during the initial phase of the war on the Eastern Front. It also served in Italy. In late 1943 the Panzerjäger was phased out of service.

PANZERJÄGER 38(T)

War on the Eastern Front presented many problems for the German Army, not least superior Soviet tanks, specifically the T-34. In the short term this was solved by the production of self-propelled antitank guns. The Panzerjäger 38(t) was one such vehicle.

As the Panzer 38(t) was obsolete as a battle tank and too slow for a reconnaissance vehicle, the chassis were singled out for conversion to gun carriages. An order dated 22 December 1941 called for production of 17 vehicles per month, beginning on 24 March 1942, with an increase to 30 units per month from July. A total of 344 were produced between April and October 1942, a further 19 Panzer 38(t) chassis being converted in 1943.

Armament consisted of the 76.2mm Pak 36(r) L/51.5 gun, which was the Russian FK296 gun rebuilt to fire the German Pak 40 cartridge. Large numbers of this weapon had been captured during the German invasion in June 1941.

The Panzerjäger 38(t) served mainly with antitank units on the Eastern Front, though 66 also served in North Africa with the 33rd and 39th Antitank Battalions. These vehicles arrived in-theatre between July and November 1942. Compared to later German antitank vehicles, the Panzerjäger 38(t) had a high silhouette and the crew was very exposed.

SPECIFICATIONS

PANZERJÄGER 38(T)

Designation: **Marder III**	Secondary Armament: **1 x 7.92mm**
Type: **SP Antitank Gun**	Engine: **Praga EPA**
Length: **5.85m (19.19ft)**	Range: **185km (116 miles)**
Width: **2.16m (7.08ft)**	Speed: **42km/h (26.25mph)**
Height: **2.5m (8.2ft)**	Fording: **.9m (3ft)**
Weight: **10,864kg (23,900lb)**	Trench Crossing: **1.87m (6.13ft)**
Crew: **Four**	Armour (hull): **50mm (1.96in)**
Main Armament: **76.2mm**	Armour (turret): **50mm (1.96in)**

PZKPFW M15/42

SPECIFICATIONS

PZKPFW M15/42

Designation: **M15/42 738(i)**	Secondary Armament: **1 x 8mm**
Type: **Medium Tank**	Engine: **15TB V-8 petrol**
Length: **5.04m (16.53ft)**	Range: **180km (112 miles)**
Width: **2.23m (7.31ft)**	Speed: **38km/h (23.75mph)**
Height: **2.39m (7.84ft)**	Fording: **1m (3.25ft)**
Weight: **14,967kg (32,928lb)**	Trench Crossing: **2.1m (6.88ft)**
Crew: **Four**	Armour (hull): **30mm (1.18in)**
Main Armament: **47mm**	Armour (turret): **49mm (1.92in)**

When the Italian Army received an updated model of its medium tank, designated M15/42, the German Army reaped the rewards. The Italians quit the Axis in September 1943 (only 82 had been delivered to the Italian Army before this date), and the German Army took control of 92 of the new tanks. Overall they still had many of the faults typical of Italian armoured fighting vehicles, but they did give the Germans some sorely needed fighting vehicles in the Italian theatre.

The Panzer M15/42 featured heavier frontal armour, a petrol-powered engine (there was a severe shortage of diesel in Italy at the time), and a longer gun. The hull length was increased to accommodate the petrol engine, while the suspension bogies were moved apart to handle the extra weight. The M15/42 was distinguished from the earlier M13/40 and M14/41 models by the location of the access door on the right-hand side of the superstructure.

In German use the M15/42 was issued to three German Army panzer detachments and the 22nd SS Division *Maria Theresia* (formed from Hungarian volunteers in April 1944). Each vehicle carried 111 rounds for the tank's 47mm KwK 47/40(i) L/40 gun, and by the end of 1944 there were still 68 Italian medium tanks in German service.

PZKPFW MKII 748 (E)

German victories in the first three years of the war resulted the capture of large numbers of enemy vehicles. These were pressed into service. The problems with this was the lack of spare parts and eventual obsolescence. Due to the small numbers involved, it was not worth the setting up of spare parts manufacture, and as a result most of these vehicles were lost due to maintenance problems. French and Italian armoured vehicles could be relatively easily maintained because those countries (which Germany occupied) had large stocks of spares, but armoured vehicles captured from other adversaries presented problems.

In North Africa, the Germans captured a large number of British armoured vehicles. They were used by the Afrika Korps until they were lost. One such vehicle was the Matilda, which in German use was designated Infanterie Panzerkampfwagen Mk II 748(e). Ironically the Germans only lost their Matildas through lack of maintenance, as no British tank then in North Africa was capable of knocking it out. In Europe, a number of captured Matildas were stripped of their turrets and converted to self-propelled guns by mounting the 50mm KwK L/42 gun. These vehicles had been captured by the Germans in 1940. However, they were only used by garrison forces stationed near the stockpiled dumps.

SPECIFICATIONS

PZKPFW MKII 748 (E)

Designation:
PzKpfw Mk II 748 (E)

Type:
Infantry Tank

Length:
5.63m (18.5ft)

Width:
2.59m (8.5ft)

Height:
2.44m (8ft)

Weight:
26,981kg (59,360lb)

Crew:
Four

Main Armament:
2pdr

Secondary Armament:
1 x 7.92mm

Engine:
Leyland diesel 190hp

Range:
257km (160 miles)

Speed:
24km/h (15mph)

Fording:
.9m (3ft)

Trench Crossing:
2.13m (7ft)

Armour (hull):
20mm (.78in)

Armour (turret):
78mm (3in)

SIG33

SPECIFICATIONS

SIG33

Designation:
sIG33 (SF)

Type:
SP Heavy Infantry Gun

Length:
4.67m (15.32ft)

Width:
2.15m (7.05ft)

Height:
2.8m (9.18ft)

Weight:
8654kg (19,040lb)

Crew:
Four

Main Armament:
150mm

Secondary Armament:
None

Engine:
Maybach NL38TR

Range:
140km (87 miles)

Speed:
40km/h (25mph)

Fording:
.9m (3ft)

Trench Crossing:
1.75m (5.74ft)

Armour (hull):
13mm (.51in)

Armour (superstructure):
13mm (.51in)

In order to give armoured infantry immediate fire support, the 150mm sIG33 L/11 heavy infantry gun was mounted on the chassis of the Panzer I Ausf B. This resulted in a self-propelled infantry gun that could follow the infantry closely into battle. The conversion was carried out by Alkett at Berlin-Spandau. The turret and superstructure of the Panzer I were removed and replaced by a large, box-shaped gun shield which was open at the rear and had an open top. The gun was placed inside the gun shield.

The sIG33 was the first of several similar improvisations the Germans made during the war, in which a gun on a standard field mounting was fitted onto a tank chassis with only slight modifications. In total 38 conversions were completed. The sIG33's gun had a traverse of 12.5 degrees to left and right and an elevation of minus four to plus 75 degrees. It was an excellent weapon that remained in service up until the end of the war in Europe.

The sIGs were used to equip 701–706 Heavy Infantry Gun Companies, which were distributed among six panzer divisions during the campaign in the Low Countries and France in May–June 1940. A number were still fighting with the 5th Panzer Division on the Eastern Front in 1943.

STUG (F1)

During World War II flamethrower tanks were popular with infantry units for a number of reasons, such as their ability to deal with enemy bunkers and strongpoints (thus saving infantry formations having to get close to such locations, which would have resulted in heavy casualties), and thus demoralise the enemy in general. It was therefore logical that the Germans would convert a number of StuGs, their prime assault gun, to flamethrowers.

In December 1942, plans were instigated to increase StuG III production by using the new chassis already on order for the Panzer III. However, with the ending of Panzer III production it was decided that of the 220 StuGs being delivered in June 1943, 10 would be converted to become Flammenwerfers (flamethrowers). From photographic evidence it appears that all these vehicles were converted from StuG III Ausf F/8s.

The conversion involved only small changes. The sturmkanone (assault gun) was replaced by a flamethrower, and fuel tanks for the weapon were also fitted. The 14mm Flammenwerfer had a traverse of 10 degrees to the left and right, with an elevation of minus 10 degrees to plus 20 degrees. The Maybach engine gave the vehicle a top speed of 40km/h (25mph), while every vehicle was equipped with a FuG5 radio.

SPECIFICATIONS

STUG (F1)

Designation:
StuG (Fl)

Type:
Flamethrower

Length:
5.52m (18.11ft)

Width:
2.95m (9.67ft)

Height:
2.16m (7ft)

Weight:
23,418kg (51,520lb)

Crew:
Four

Main Armament:
14mm Flammenwerfer

Secondary Armament:
1 x 7.92mm

Engine:
Maybach HL120TRM

Range:
155km (97 miles)

Speed:
40km/h (25mph)

Fording:
.8m (2.62ft)

Trench Crossing:
2.59m (8.49ft)

Armour (hull):
50mm (1.96in)

Armour (superstructure):
50mm (1.96in)

STUG III AUSF B

SPECIFICATIONS

STUG III AUSF B

Designation:
SdKfz 142

Type:
Assault Gun

Length:
5.4m (17.71ft)

Width:
2.95m (9.67ft)

Height:
1.98m (6.49ft)

Weight:
20,567kg (45,248lb)

Crew:
Four

Main Armament:
75mm

Secondary Armament:
None

Engine:
Maybach HL120TRM

Range:
160km (100 miles)

Speed:
40km/h (25mph)

Fording:
.8m (2.62ft)

Trench Crossing:
2.59m (8.49ft)

Armour (hull):
50mm (1.96in)

Armour (superstructure):
50mm (1.96in)

The Sturmgeschütz (assault gun) – an armoured self-propelled gun to support infantry assaults – was first requested in 1936. The chassis of the Panzer III was selected for the assault gun, with the first gun being the 75mm StuK37 L/24. In the quest for a low silhouette an all-round traverse was abandoned. Fitted low in the hull front plate, the gun had a 12-degree traverse to the left and right, and an elevation of 10 degrees and a depression of 10 degrees.

The Ausf B was armed with the short-barrelled 75mm StuK37 L/24 gun, and had an improved ignition system, with a synchromesh transmission replacing the pre-selective type used in the Ausf A. Some Ausf Bs were fitted with a new six-spoke drive sprocket, plus an eight-spoke idler for the wider tracks.

The StuG III was first used in small numbers during the campaign in the West in 1940, and by the end of the year 184 had been produced, with a further 548 in 1941. A total of 320 Ausf B variants were built between June 1940 and May 1941. In early 1941 the German Army formed additional assault artillery detachments, which were equipped with Ausf Bs. They were used in the Balkans in the spring of 1941 and then during the invasion of the Soviet Union in the June of that year. Most were destroyed on the Eastern Front.

STUG III AUSF G

In December 1942, the first of the final production series of the StuG III – the Ausf G – rolled off the production line in Germany. When production ceased in March 1945, a total of 7720 had been built. The hull of the Ausf G was not radically different from previous models, the main changes being to the superstructure. A cupola with periscopes was added for the commander, while a shield for the machine gun was installed in front of the loader's hatch.

The superstructure incorporated slanted sides, with the addition of slanted plates to protect the front of both panniers. During the production run other changes were incorporated, such as the introduction of the "sow's head" (Saukopf) gun mantlet for the StuK40 L/48 gun, a coaxial machine gun in early 1944, a close-in defence weapon, and a remote-controlled machine gun to the superstructure roof in the spring of 1944.

By mid-1943, there were 28 independent StuG detachments, four divisional StuG detachments, two radio-controlled companies, and 12 StuG platoons, all ready for the Kursk Offensive in July. Later, the StuGs were distributed among panzer and antitank units. The illustration above shows an Ausf G fitted with a Saukopf gun mantlet and the machine-gun shield in front of the loader's hatch.

SPECIFICATIONS

STUG III AUSF G

Designation: **SdKfz 142/1**	Secondary Armament: **2 x 7.92mm**
Type: **Assault Gun**	Engine: **Maybach HL120TRM**
Length: **6.77m (22.21ft)**	Range: **155km (97 miles)**
Width: **2.95m (9.67ft)**	Speed: **40km/h (25mph)**
Height: **2.16m (7.08ft)**	Fording: **.8m (2.62ft)**
Weight: **24,334kg (53,536lb)**	Trench Crossing: **2.59m (8.49ft)**
Crew: **Four**	Armour (hull): **80mm (3.14in)**
Main Armament: **75mm**	Armour (superstructure): **80mm (3.14in)**

TIGER I

SPECIFICATIONS

TIGER I

Designation: **SdKfz 181**	Secondary Armament: **2 x 7.92mm**
Type: **Heavy Tank**	Engine: **Maybach HL210P45**
Length: **8.45m (27.72ft)**	Range: **140km (87.5 miles)**
Width: **3.7m (12.13ft)**	Speed: **38km/h (23.75mph)**
Height: **2.93m (9.61ft)**	Fording: **1.56m (5.1ft)**
Weight: **57,000kg (125,400lb)**	Trench Crossing: **2.29m (7.51ft)**
Crew: **Five**	Armour (hull): **100mm (3.93in)**
Main Armament: **88mm**	Armour (turret): **100mm (3.93in)**

The Tiger I originated from competition between Henschel, Porsche, MAN and Daimler-Benz to produce a heavy tank. The winner was Henschel, and the new vehicle entered production in August 1942. It was the first tank to be fitted with an overlapping road wheel suspension, arranged with triple overlapping and interleaved steel wheels. The Tiger had eight independently sprung torsion bar axles on each side. The result was a very stable and soft ride for such a large tank. However, the interleaved wheels became clogged with mud in wet conditions, which then jammed the wheels if temperatures dropped below freezing.

The hull was divided into four compartments: the forward two housed the driver and hull gunner/radio operator; the centre was the fighting compartment, and the engine compartment was at the rear. To simplify assembly and allow the use of armour plate, flat sections were use throughout the hull. The ballistic characteristics of the KwK 36 gun were similar to the famous "88" anti-aircraft gun. The main modifications were the addition of a muzzle brake and electric firing. Early Tigers were fitted with "S" mine dischargers (though from 1943 a close-defence weapon was fitted in the turret roof), and were equipped with snorkels for submerged wading. Some 1354 Tiger I's were produced to August 1943.

TIGER II

The result of a German Army Weapons Office demand for a redesigned Tiger with thicker armour, sloped plates and a powerful gun, the Tiger Ausf B, or "King Tiger", entered production in December 1943. Henschel was the sole manufacturer of the vehicle, though the first 50 Tiger IIs completed mounted the turret of the rival Porsche design (with a curved front mantlet and a bulged commander's cupola). Suspension was similar to the Tiger I, but the wheels were overlapped rather than interleaved to simplify maintenance problems. LIke the Tiger I, the arrangement gave good cross-country performance despite the vehicle's weight.

The Tiger II incorporated design features resulting from battle experience. The front plate, for example, was 150mm (5.9in) thick and set at an angle of 40 degrees, rather than squarely vertical as on the Tiger I, making it invulnerable to any enemy antitank weapon. Its KwK 43 L/71 gun was extremely potent and the vehicles were often covered with anti-magnetic Zimmerit paste to defeat magnetic mines.

However, the Tiger II suffered from mechanical problems (many broke down and had to be abandoned by their crews) during the war and its low speed was a handicap in battle. Production ceased in March 1945, by which time a total of 489 had been built.

SPECIFICATIONS

TIGER II

Designation:
SdKfz 182

Type:
Heavy Tank

Length:
10.3m (33.79ft)

Width:
3.76m (12.33ft)

Height:
3.08m (10.1ft)

Weight:
70,000kg (154,000lb)

Crew:
Five

Main Armament:
88mm

Secondary Armament:
2 x 7.92mm

Engine:
Maybach HL230P30

Range:
170km (106 miles)

Speed:
42km/h (26.25mph)

Fording:
1.63m (5.24ft)

Trench Crossing:
3m (9.84ft)

Armour (hull):
100mm (3.93in)

Armour (turret):
180mm (7in)

WESPE

SPECIFICATIONS

WESPE

Designation:
SdKfz 124

Type:
SP Light Field Howitzer

Length:
4.81m (15.78ft)

Width:
2.28m (7.48ft)

Height:
2.3m (7.54ft)

Weight:
13,300kg (29,260lb)

Crew:
Five

Main Armament:
105mm

Secondary Armament:
1 x 7.92mm

Engine:
Maybach HL62TR

Range:
220km (137 miles)

Speed:
40km/h (25mph)

Fording:
.85m (2.78ft)

Trench Crossing:
1.75m (5.74ft)

Armour (hull):
30mm (1.18in)

Armour (superstructure):
20mm (.78in)

In the search for a platform to carry the 105mm leFH18M L/28 howitzer, the chassis of the Panzer II was preferred over those of the Panzer III and IV. The first Wespes proved a great success, and so all Panzer II chassis production was ordered to be used for their manufacture.

The Wespe was built on a modified Panzer II chassis with the hull lengthened, the engine moved forward, the cooling system louvres redesigned, and the glacis extended. The number of return rollers on the suspension was reduced from four to three, while spring bumper stops were added for the road wheels to absorb recoil. The driver was separated from the rest of the crew, sitting in a small compartment in the front next to the transmission. A total of 32 rounds of ammunition were carried for the main gun.

Between February 1943 and July 1943, 676 Wespes were produced, with a further 159 munitions vehicles manufactured during the same period (these vehicles were also designed to mount the field howitzer when other Wespes became unserviceable or were disabled). The Wespe was issued to panzer and panzergrenadier divisions, its first major action being at the disastrous Battle of Kursk in mid-1943. Thereafter, it served on all fronts up to the end of the war.

CENTURION

The Centurion began life as an idea in 1943 for a heavy cruiser tank able to defeat, by the time it went into production, any German tank in its class. The aim was to have the first models ready by the end of 1944, with production starting in the second quarter of 1945. Its main armament would consist of a 17-pounder gun with a coaxial machine gun, with the ability to up-gun to a 32-pounder if required.

Production began in May 1945, and six prototypes were rushed to the front in Germany. However, the war ended before the Centurion could be tested under combat conditions. An alternative auxiliary armament was a coaxial 20mm cannon, but this was soon dropped as its ammunition took up too much internal space.

The main features of the Centurion included armoured side skirts, and a Horstmann suspension replacing that of the Christie design used on previous cruiser tank designs. Other new features were a cast turret and sloping glacis plate. In the Centurion the British had a tank that was on an almost equal footing with the best the Germans could field, especially as it fired armoured-piercing, discarding sabot rounds. It was also reliable and well-armoured. Testimony to the Centurion's effectiveness is that after 1945 it was developed through 13 basic marks with many sub-variants and special purpose vehicles.

SPECIFICATIONS

CENTURION

Designation: **Cruiser Tank Centurion**	Secondary Armament: **2 x 7.92mm**
Type: **Heavy Cruiser Tank**	Engine: **Meteor 620hp**
Length: **7.66m (12.16ft)**	Range: **205km (127 miles)**
Width: **3.39m (11.12ft)**	Speed: **32.24km/h (21.4mph)**
Height: **2.92m (9.6ft)**	Fording: **1.45m (4.75ft)**
Weight: **51,723kg (113,792lb)**	Trench Crossing: **3.35m (11ft)**
Crew: **Four**	Armour (hull): **51mm (.97in)**
Main Armament: **17pdr**	Armour (turret): **152mm (5.98in)**

CHURCHILL

SPECIFICATIONS

CHURCHILL

Designation:
Infantry Tank Mk IV

Type:
Infantry Tank

Length:
7.46m (24.5ft)

Width:
2.43m (7.97ft)

Height:
2.74m (9ft)

Weight:
40,727kg (89,600lb)

Crew:
Five

Main Armament:
75mm

Secondary Armament:
2 x 7.92mm

Engine:
Bedford 350hp

Range:
145km (90 miles)

Speed:
24.8km/h (15.5mph)

Fording:
1.01m (3.31ft)

Trench Crossing:
3.04m (10ft)

Armour (hull):
25mm (.98in)

Armour (turret):
102mm (4in)

Originally designed as a "shelled area" tank, the Churchill was intended to fight on the Western Front, which at the beginning of World War II was envisaged as being similar to the conditions experienced in World War I. First production models were delivered in 1941, but they were plagued by mechanical faults and these had to be rectified before work could continue.

Notwithstanding these difficulties (which were ironed out), the Churchill went on to become one of the most successful British tank designs of the war. It served in a variety of roles, including close-support, engineer vehicle, carpet layer, anti-mine vehicle and flamethrower.

The Churchill had a squared-off shape with overall tracks, spacious side panniers, small road wheels, very heavy armour and a slow speed. These qualities made it an excellent platform for the attachment of special purpose equipment, such as ploughs and demolition frames. The first models were armed with a two-pounder or six-pounder gun, but later Churchills carried the more formidable 75mm gun.

The Churchill Crocodile was a Mk VII tank armed with a 75mm gun, coaxial machine gun in the turret and a flame projector in the hull. It towed an armoured trailer containing fuel for the flame projector. If set on fire, the trailer could be jettisoned by a quick-release gear.

COMET

In 1943, work began on developing a successor to the Cromwell and Challenger tanks, under the General Staff specification A34. The design was based on technology used in the Cromwell, and it was intended that the new vehicle would be armed with the Vickers 75mm gun. However, for reasons of communality the 17-pounder model was chosen, being modified by Vickers. The weapon was designated as the "Gun, QF, Tank 77mm". The title "77mm" was adopted to avoid confusion with other 3in guns which were entering British and US service.

Production of the Comet began in the autumn of 1944, and by January 1945 143 vehicles had been built. Comprising an all-welded hull and a turret which was part cast and part rolled plate, it was mechanically identical to the Cromwell. Though slower than the latter, its main gun was more powerful then the Cromwell's, especially when firing the new armoured-piercing, discarding sabot round, which had a muzzle velocity of 1097m/sec (3600ft/sec).

The Comet saw action in Germany in March–May 1945, right at the end of the war in Europe, and was judged a great success, being more reliable than either the Challenger or Cromwell. The Comet remained in British Army service until the mid-1960s.

SPECIFICATIONS

COMET

Designation:
Cruiser Tank Comet

Type:
Heavy Cruiser Tank

Length:
7.65m (25.1ft)

Width:
3.04m (10ft)

Height:
2.66m (8.75ft)

Weight:
33,090kg (72,800lb)

Crew:
Five

Main Armament:
77mm

Secondary Armament:
2 x 7.92mm

Engine:
Meteor 600hp

Range:
250km (156.25 miles)

Speed:
18km/h (29mph)

Fording:
1.12m (4ft)

Trench Crossing:
2.28m (7.5ft)

Armour (hull):
25mm (.98in)

Armour (turret):
101mm (3.97in)

CROMWELL

SPECIFICATIONS

CROMWELL

Designation:
Cruiser Tank Mk VIII

Type:
Cruiser Tank

Length:
6.33m (20.8ft)

Width:
3.04m (10ft)

Height:
2.5 m (8.2ft)

Weight:
28,509kg (67,720lb)

Crew:
Five

Main Armament:
75mm

Secondary Armament:
1 x 7.92mm

Engine:
Meteor 600hp

Range:
278km (173 miles)

Speed:
64km/h (40mph)

Fording:
1.21m (4ft)

Trench Crossing:
2.28m (7.5ft)

Armour (hull):
8mm (.31in)

Armour (turret):
76mm (2.99in)

British cruiser tanks were designed to be relatively fast and lightly armoured to assume the cavalry role on the battlefield: to exploit gaps punched in enemy defences by the heavier infantry tanks, and then penetrate far behind enemy lines in the way horsed cavalry did in earlier periods.

There were a number of cruiser tanks manufactured by the British. Two versions of the Cruiser Tank Mk VIII developed were the A27L (Centaur) and the A27M Cromwell. Designed by the Birmingham Railway Carriage and Wagon Company, the Cromwell was powered by the new Rolls-Royce Meteor engine (hence the "M" in the designation).

The design of the tank is interesting. It had first been drawn up in 1940, and as a result of experience in the North African war some outmoded construction practices and design features were included. These included a slab-sided hull and turret in preference to sloped armour, a bolted and riveted design rather than welded, and a shoulder-controlled main gun/coaxial armament rather than a mechanical geared system. The shoulder-controlled system had been introduced in the 1930s as a means of firing relatively accurately on the move (with slow tanks it was adequate enough, but it was woefully deficient when tank speeds increased).

CROMWELL MK VI

By the time of the invasion of France in June 1944, the Cromwell was the most important British tank in service. Fast and well armed, it was still under-armed when compared to the fearsome German Panthers and Tigers it came into contact with in Normandy. Nevertheless, it was reliable and by equipping their armoured reconnaissance units with Cromwells the British in effect added an extra medium tank battalion to their armoured divisions.

Fast the Cromwell may have been, but when it came to tank-versus-tank action it suffered alarmingly. An example was Operation Goodwood, launched in Normandy on 18 July 1944, during which an estimated 1350 British tanks came to blows with 400 German armoured vehicles (most of which were in hull-down positions). It has been described as a "tactical holocaust", and indeed losses were fearful. German tanks, firing from good positions at optimum ranges, destroyed 300 British tanks in 72 hours.

The Cromwell had been produced in large numbers, with manufacture beginning in 1943. The above illustration shows the Cromwell VI close-support version armed with a 95mm howitzer. And, despite its overall shortcomings, the Cromwell VI and VIII remained in service with British Army regiments until the 1950s.

SPECIFICATIONS

CROMWELL MK VI

Designation:
Cruiser Tank Mk VI

Type:
Cruiser Tank

Length:
6.33m (20.8ft)

Width:
3.04m (10ft)

Height:
2.5 m (8.2ft)

Weight:
28,509kg (67,720lb)

Crew:
Five

Main Armament:
95mm

Secondary Armament:
1 x 7.92mm

Engine:
Meteor 600hp

Range:
250km (156.25 miles)

Speed:
64km/h (40mph)

Fording:
1.21m (4ft)

Trench Crossing:
2.28m (7.5ft)

Armour (hull):
8mm (.31in)

Armour (turret):
76mm (2.99in)

CHALLENGER

SPECIFICATIONS

CHALLENGER

Designation:
Cruiser Tank Challenger

Type:
Cruiser Tank

Length:
8m (26.3ft)

Width:
2.89m (9.5ft)

Height:
2.66m (8.75ft)

Weight:
32,581kg (71,680lb)

Crew:
Five

Main Armament:
17pdr

Secondary Armament:
1 x 7.92mm

Engine:
Meteor 600hp

Range:
260km (162.5 miles)

Speed:
51km/h (32mph)

Fording:
1.21m (4ft)

Trench Crossing:
2.28m (7.5ft)

Armour (hull):
20mm (.78in)

Armour (turret):
102mm (4in)

The Challenger was the result of a further development of the Cromwell tank under the General Staff Specification A30. It was designed to mount the new 17-pounder high-velocity antitank gun, and it came into service in 1944.

It had been originally thought that the Centaur/Comet chassis could used for the Challenger, but weight and size of the gun and turret meant a redesigned chassis. The result was a longer, wider vehicle with a high turret, very long gun, widened centre hull and Christie suspension. Some 200 were built in total, 12 being allocated to each armoured regiment, and they saw limited service in Europe in 1944–45.

Great things were expected of the Challenger, but in service it proved something of a disappointment. It was under-armoured and difficult to steer due to its increased length (there was no corresponding increase in width between track centres, thus the ratio of length to width was increased to unacceptable levels). In addition, the Challenger was unable to engage the Panther and Tiger on equal terms. A parallel development – the mounting of the 17-pounder in the Sherman – proved more of a success, and the resultant vehicle, the Sherman Firefly, ultimately took over the role envisaged for the Challenger.

CRUISER TANK MK I

The early British tanks in the cruiser category did not have names, but were merely known by their General Staff designation ("A") numbers. The A9, together with the A10 and A13, was one of first to reach the army in 1938.

The main armament of the A9 was the two-pounder gun, which was the standard armament of all British cruiser and infantry tanks up to 1942. In 1930 the two-pounder was reckoned to be one of the best tank guns in the world, though it was rapidly outclassed as the war progressed. To increase its armour penetration, it was fitted with a Littlejohn squeeze muzzle attachment for firing armour-piercing, composite non-rigid rounds. However, this provided only a temporary respite.

The design of the A9 was unusual, and incorporated three-wheel bogies, power traverse for the turret, and two auxiliary machine-gun turrets. Machine guns initially consisted of .303in Vickers water-cooled guns coaxially with the main gun, with two other .303in Vickers in the turrets. It shared the same Carden-designed running gear, engine, transmission and main armament found in the A10 and A13. The hull was essentially an oblong box carried between the tracks. The A9 was in service 1938–41. Despite its innovative design, it was too lightly armed to take on comparable German tanks.

SPECIFICATIONS

CRUISER TANK MK I

Designation: **Cruiser Tank Mk I (A9)**	Secondary Armament: **3 x .330in**
Type: **Cruiser Tank**	Engine: **AEG 150hp**
Length: **5.86m (19.25ft)**	Range: **210km (131.25 miles)**
Width: **2.53m (8.33ft)**	Speed: **40km/h (25mph)**
Height: **2.52m (8.3ft)**	Fording: **.9m (3ft)**
Weight: **12,218kg (26,880lb)**	Trench Crossing: **2.26m (7.41ft)**
Crew: **Six**	Armour (hull): **6mm (.23in)**
Main Armament: **2pdr**	Armour (turret): **14mm (.55in)**

CRUISER TANK MK IV

SPECIFICATIONS

CRUISER TANK MK IV

Designation:
Cruiser Tank Mk IV

Type:
Cruiser Tank

Length:
6m (19.75ft)

Width:
2.53m (8.33ft)

Height:
2.59m (8.5ft)

Weight:
14,254kg (31,360lb)

Crew:
Four

Main Armament:
2pdr

Secondary Armament:
1 x .303in

Engine:
Liberty 340hp

Range:
232km (144 miles)

Speed:
48km/h (30mph)

Fording:
.9m (3ft)

Trench Crossing:
2.26m (7.41ft)

Armour (hull):
6mm (.23in)

Armour (turret):
30mm (1.18in)

The Cruiser Tank Mk IV (A13) originated in 1936 following British War Office observers witnessing the high speed of the Christie-type BT tanks in Soviet service. The Nuffield company was therefore asked to design a tank based on the Christie design to replace the A9 and A10.

The resulting Cruiser Tank Mk III had high speed, Christie suspension and a high power-to-weight ratio. The Mk IV was an up-armoured version of the Mk III, with the addition of extra armoured plates and an armour thickness of 20-30mm (.78-1.18in). The Mk IV was in production by 1938, and was used by the British Expeditionary Force (BEF) in France in 1940.

The distinctive design feature of the A13 tanks was their flat-sided turrets. Another design feature was different-shaped mantlets. The Cruiser Tank Mk IVA had an axle-shaped mantlet, while other Mk IVs had rectangular-shaped mantlets. All the Cruiser Tanks went to France with the BEF with high hopes. However, once they got there their performance left a lot to be desired. They were found to be unreliable, underpowered, under-armoured and had tracks that were too narrow and came off too easily. That said, in North Africa in 1941 their performance improved (no doubt a dryer climate and regular maintenance were the reasons).

CRUISER TANK MK V

The Mk V Covenanter was designed to use as many parts of the A13 as possible. The new vehicle was designated the A13 Mk III, Cruiser Tank Mk V, and immediately it had a host of problems. They were mainly to do with the engine, which was the only untried feature. The cooling system was particularly irksome, and required army workshops modifying the engine air intake louvres, which were located at the front left-hand side, next to the driver. The tanks thus modified were known as Covenanter Mk IIs.

The Covenanter was in service by 1940, and in 1941 two further models appeared – the Mk III and IV – but the cooling system problem was never properly resolved and so the Covenanter was finally declared unfit for overseas service.

Despite its shortcomings, the Covenanter played an important part in the defence of Great Britain, first helping to re-equip those units that had lost their tanks in the defeat in France in 1940 (the British Army had left nearly all of its heavy equipment behind during the evacuation from Dunkirk), and then contributing to the new armoured divisions being raised. The 9th Armoured Division, for example, was almost exclusively equipped with Covenanters. Despite its problems, 1771 vehicles were built and they saw home service up to 1943.

SPECIFICATIONS

CRUISER TANK MK V

Designation: **Cruiser Tank Mk V**	Secondary Armament: **1 x 7.92mm**
Type: **Cruiser Tank**	Engine: **Meadows Flat-12 300hp**
Length: **5.79m (19ft)**	Range: **200km (125 miles)**
Width: **2.62m (8.6ft)**	Speed: **50km/h (31mph)**
Height: **2.22m (7.3ft)**	Fording: **1m (3.25ft)**
Weight: **18,327kg (40,320lb)**	Trench Crossing: **1.52m (4.98ft)**
Crew: **Four**	Armour (hull): **7mm (.27in)**
Main Armament: **2pdr**	Armour (turret): **40mm (1.57in)**

CRUISER TANK MK VII

SPECIFICATIONS

CRUISER TANK MK VII

Designation: **Cruiser Tank Mk VII**	Secondary Armament: **2 x 7.92mm**
Type: **Cruiser Tank**	Engine: **Liberty 410hp**
Length: **6.33m (19.8ft)**	Range: **200km (125 miles)**
Width: **2.89m (9.5ft)**	Speed: **38.4km/h (24mph)**
Height: **2.4m (8ft)**	Fording: **1m (3.25ft)**
Weight: **26,981kg (59,360lb)**	Trench Crossing: **2.59m (8.49ft)**
Crew: **Five**	Armour (hull): **20mm (.78in)**
Main Armament: **6pdr**	Armour (turret): **76mm (3in)**

An enlarged version of the Covenanter was the A13 Mk III, which was called the Crusader. By late 1942 this tank was obsolete, and so was temporarily succeeded by the Cruiser Tank Mk VII (A24). This vehicle was originally named the Cromwell I, but was later renamed the Cavalier.

The tank had the six-pounder as its main armament, which was an effective antitank weapon when it entered service (though it lacked a high-explosive round throughout most of its service life), with a coaxial BESA machine gun plus another BESA in the hull. The 7.92mm BESA was built under licence by the company BSA. It was developed from the Czech ZB37, and was an accurate and reliable weapon, though rather bulky for a tank and requiring a large opening in the tank's armour. Nevertheless, it was the standard British armoured fighting vehicle armament in World War II.

The Cavalier was an interim until the Cromwell was developed, and because of this only 50 were built. These were used for training purposes only. Externally the Cavalier was almost identical to the Centaur and Cavalier, with Christie suspension and rectangular hull and turret. The Cavalier entered service in 1942 and continued in its training role until the end of the war, providing a valuable role of familiarization.

CRUSADER III

Designed and manufactured by Nuffield Mechanisation & Aero, the Cruiser Tank Mk VI (A15) Crusader was, like the Covenanter, armed with the two-pounder main gun. Auxiliary weapons consisted of two 7.92mm BESA machine guns, one mounted coaxially with the main gun and the other in a small turret on the forward hull roof, next to the driver.

The Crusader design shared many common components with the Covenanter. It was ordered in July 1939, and became one of the main British tanks until production ceased in 1943. By that time numbers built totalled 5300.

The Crusader was used extensively in the North African war, where it suffered from a number of mechanical problems. In addition, the Crusader's light armour was also a major disadvantage when it came up against German panzers. The Crusader was produced in a number of variants. The Crusader I CS was a close-support model armed with a 3in howitzer in place of the two-pounder gun. The Crusader II had additional armour, while the Crusader II CS was again a close-support vehicle armed with the 3in howitzer. The Crusader III, illustrated above, was the final production model and was armed with the six-pounder main gun in place of the two-pounder.

SPECIFICATIONS

CRUSADER III

Designation:
Cruiser Tank Mk VI

Type:
Cruiser Tank

Length:
6m (19.68ft)

Width:
2.64m (8.66ft)

Height:
2.23m (7.31ft)

Weight:
20,067kg (44,147lb)

Crew:
Three

Main Armament:
6pdr

Secondary Armament:
2 x 7.92mm

Engine:
Nuffield Liberty 340hp

Range:
204km (127 miles)

Speed:
50km/h (31mph)

Fording:
.9m (3.25ft)

Trench Crossing:
2.59m (8.49ft)

Armour (hull):
7mm (.27in)

Armour (turret):
40mm (1.57in)

GRANT MEDIUM TANK

SPECIFICATIONS

GRANT MEDIUM TANK

Designation:
Grant Medium Tank

Secondary Armament:
1 x 37mm

Type:
Medium Tank

Engine:
Wright Continental R-975

Length:
5.63m (18.5ft)

Range:
257km (160 miles)

Width:
2.51m (8.5ft)

Speed:
41.6km/h (26mph)

Height:
2.81m (9.25ft)

Fording:
1.02m (3.34ft)

Weight:
27,272kg (60,000lb)

Trench Crossing:
1.91m (6.26ft)

Crew:
Six

Armour (hull):
38.1mm (1.5in)

Main Armament:
75mm

Armour (turret):
12.7mm (.5in)

Under the terms of the Lend-Lease scheme, the British purchased a number of Medium Tank M3s from the US government. The vehicle was slightly modified, as the British Tank Commission requested a modification to suit British requirements. This entailed changes to the turret, which was longer than the M3 version, with a prominent rear overhang to allow for the installation of wireless equipment in the turret rear.

The vehicle's silhouette, somewhat high, was reduced by doing away with the cupola, and the turret itself was reduced by at least 305mm (12in) – although the end result was still an excellent target for antitank gunners. The M3 was a vehicle of necessity, as the Americans produced it believing that future tanks would require a main gun of not less than 75mm calibre, but at the time – 1941 – they were unable to produce a fully rotating turret to house such a weapon. Thus the 75mm gun was housed in a hull sponson, while the rotating turret housed a 37mm gun.

The M3 in British service was known as the Grant after the American Civil War general U.S. Grant. The Grant Canal Defence Light version was not a tank but an armoured housing with a powerful searchlight in the place of the original tank turret to light up the battlefield during night actions.

INFANTRY TANK MK II

The Infantry Tank Mk II Matilda was designed as an immediate replacement for the Infantry Tank Mk I, Matilda I, as the latter was totally inadequate for its intended role. The prototype was first tested in April 1938, and it proved to be one of the best tanks at this time. However, it was a complicated tank and not really suited to mass production. The fact that only two were in service when war broke out in September 1939 is testament to its production problems.

The tank's main armament was the two-pounder gun, with a coaxial BESA machine gun and two single-shot smoke bomb throwers mounted externally on the turret side and operated by cable from within the turret. The Matilda was relatively small, but because of its heavy cast hull and side skirts it appeared massive. Some 2987 were produced between 1940 and 1943, some being sent as aid to the Soviet Union.

In service the Matilda proved useful. In France, in 1940, German 37mm antitank rounds bounced off its hull, and in North Africa in 1940 it helped to smash Italian artillery and armour. There were also a number of special purpose derivatives built, such as the Matilda Scorpion, a tank flail device designed to clear a path through enemy minefields by beating on the ground as the vehicle advanced.

SPECIFICATIONS

INFANTRY TANK MK II

Designation:
Infantry Tank Mk II

Type:
Infantry Tank

Length:
5.63m (18.5ft)

Width:
2.59m (8.5ft)

Height:
2.44m (8ft)

Weight:
26,981kg (59,360lb)

Crew:
Four

Main Armament:
2pdr

Secondary Armament:
1 x 7.92mm

Engine:
Leyland Diesel 190hp

Range:
257km (160 miles)

Speed:
24km/h (15mph)

Fording:
.9m (3ft)

Trench Crossing:
2.13m (7ft)

Armour (hull):
20mm (.78in)

Armour (turret):
78mm (3in)

LIGHT TANK MK VI

SPECIFICATIONS

LIGHT TANK MK VI

Designation: **Light Tank Mk VI**	**Secondary Armament:** **None**
Type: **Light Tank**	**Engine:** **Meadows ESTB/A 88hp**
Length: **4.02m (13.2ft)**	**Range:** **200km (125 miles)**
Width: **2.08m (6.83ft)**	**Speed:** **56km/h (35mph)**
Height: **2.28m (7.5ft)**	**Fording:** **.9m (3ft)**
Weight: **5294kg (11,648lb)**	**Trench Crossing:** **1.52m (4.98ft)**
Crew: **Three**	**Armour (hull):** **4mm (.15in)**
Main Armament: **1 x .303in, 1 x .5in**	**Armour (turret):** **14mm (.59in)**

Designed by Vickers Armstrong Ltd, the Light Tank Mk VI was the culmination of a long series of Light Tanks stemming from the Carden-Loyd Mk VIII. It followed the pattern of its predecessors and had its engine in the right-hand side of the hull, with the transmission led forward to drive the front sprockets. The driver sat in the left-hand side, while the turret, containing the commander and gunner, was also off-set to the left.

The suspension consisted of two-wheeled bogie units each side, sprung on twin coil springs, the rear wheel acting also as a trailing idler. This arrangement was simple and dependable, though the tracks had a nasty tendency to shed themselves at speed.

Armament consisted of two machine guns – a Vickers .5in and a water-cooled .303in Vickers – and armour thickness was poor. The Mk VI was actually no more than a reconnaissance vehicle, though the British Army used it as a battle tank in 1940 because of the delay in the delivery of Cruiser tanks. Needless to say, they were no match for the German tanks they came up against in France, and suffered accordingly. Mk VIBs and earlier light tanks were also used in the early campaigns in North Africa, where they fared better against equally poor Italian tanks.

MEDIUM TANK MK II

The Medium Tank Mk II first appeared in 1925, being more heavily armoured than the Mk I and its suspension being protected by armoured side skirts. When it first appeared it was a formidable armoured fighting vehicle, and was actually a world leader in tank design. The Mk II was in service until 1939 and was thereafter used for training purposes.

The Mk II* had a coaxial Vickers machine gun in the turret but no Hotchkiss machine guns, though a commander's cupola was added. The Mk II** was a Mk II conversion, having twin mountings for the three-pounder gun and a Vickers .303in machine gun. Some 44 vehicles were thus converted. The Medium Tank Mk IIA was produced in 1930 by Vickers Armstrong Ltd, but only 20 were built. The bevel was removed from the rear of the turret and a command cupola was fitted. Other modifications included better suspension units with rearranged track-return rollers.

A close-support version was the Medium Tank Mk IIA CS, which was armed with a 3.7in howitzer. Five tanks were converted for service in tropical conditions, having sun screens consisting of woven asbestos. They were fitted outside the upper surfaces and sides of the tank. The bridge-laying version of the tank was fitted with side brackets to carry bridge girders.

SPECIFICATIONS

MEDIUM TANK MK II

Designation:
Medium Tank Mk II

Type:
Medium Tank

Length:
5.33m (17.5ft)

Width:
2.77m (9.1ft)

Height:
2.68m (8.8ft)

Weight:
13,440kg (29,568lb)

Crew:
Five

Main Armament:
3pdr

Secondary Armament:
6 x .303in

Engine:
Armstrong-Siddeley 90hp

Range:
257km (160 miles)

Speed:
24km/h (15mph)

Fording:
.85m (2.9ft)

Trench Crossing:
1.75m (5.75ft)

Armour (hull):
8.25mm (.32in)

Armour (turret):
8.25mm (.32in)

SHERMAN FIREFLY

SPECIFICATIONS

SHERMAN FIREFLY

Designation:
Sherman Firefly

Type:
Medium Tank

Length:
6.27m (20.57ft)

Width:
2.68m (8.79ft)

Height:
3.43m (11.25ft)

Weight:
32,284kg (71,024lb)

Crew:
Five

Main Armament:
17pdr

Secondary Armament:
1 x .3in, 1 x .5in

Engine:
Ford V-8 500hp

Range:
160km (100 miles)

Speed:
47km/h (29mph)

Fording:
.9m (3ft)

Trench Crossing:
2.26m (7.41ft)

Armour (hull):
15mm (.59in)

Armour (turret):
100mm (3.93in)

In 1943 it was decided to mount the British high-velocity 17-pounder gun in the Sherman medium tank to give the vehicle some "punch" against German Tigers and Panthers. This required the turret being modified and the gun being mounted on its side and adapted for left-hand loading.

The gun filled most of the turret, so an aperture had to be cut in the rear of the turret and an armoured box was added. This acted as a counterweight and contained the tank's radio sets. An additional hatch for the loader was cut in the turret roof, as the gun breech obstructed his exit through the commander's rotating roof hatch. To make room inside the hull, the hull gunner's position was done away with, the bow machine gun was removed, the aperture plated over and an ammunition bin replaced the seat. Each vehicle could thus carry 78 rounds for the main gun.

Most Fireflies were converted from Sherman Vs. The Ordnance, QF, 17-pounder was originally developed as a towed antitank gun. It was too heavy for manhandling in the field, and was too large for mounting in British tanks when it entered service in 1942. It was mounted on the Cruiser, though with some difficulty, but was more easily adapted for the Sherman, and some 600 of the latter vehicles were so modified.

VALENTINE II

Because the proposal for this infantry tank was sent to the War Office just before St. Valentine's Day 1938, it was named after the saint's day thereafter. The Valentine was in fact one of the most reliable of British tanks, being based on the A9 and A10 tanks. Both hull and turret were more compact, but this limited the vehicle to a three-man crew.

The first contract, for 275 tanks, was placed with Vickers Armstrong, with a further 125 being ordered from the Metropolitan-Cammell Carriage & Wagon Company Ltd and 200 more from the Birmingham Railway Carriage & Wagon Company Ltd. When war broke out Valentine production rose steadily, and by mid-1941 they were being delivered at a rate of 45 per month. They were issued in lieu of Cruiser tanks to equip some of the new armoured divisions that were formed after the Dunkirk evacuation.

The Valentine was developed through several models. The Mk I was the original vehicle; the Mk II had an AEC six-cylinder engine instead of the petrol one. Armament for the early Valentines consisted of a two-pounder gun. Though home defence was the primary role of the tank in 1940–41, some were sent to North Africa at the end of 1941. A total of 8275 had been built by the time production ceased in 1944.

SPECIFICATIONS

VALENTINE II

Designation: **Infantry Tank Mk III**	Secondary Armament: **1 x 7.92mm**
Type: **Infantry Tank**	Engine: **GM diesel 138hp**
Length: **5.41m (17.75ft)**	Range: **145km (90 miles)**
Width: **2.62m (8.59ft)**	Speed: **24km/h (15mph)**
Height: **2.28m (7.5ft)**	Fording: **.9m (3ft)**
Weight: **17,309kg (38,080lb)**	Trench Crossing: **2.28m (7.48ft)**
Crew: **Three**	Armour (hull): **8mm (.31in)**
Main Armament: **2pdr**	Armour (turret): **65mm (2.55in)**

CARRO ARMATO M11/39

SPECIFICATIONS

CARRO ARMATO M11/39

Designation:
Carro Armato M11/39

Type:
Medium Tank

Length:
4.72m (15.5ft)

Width:
2.15m (7.08ft)

Height:
2.23m (7.33ft)

Weight:
11,200 kg (24,640lb)

Crew:
Three

Main Armament:
37mm

Secondary Armament:
2 x 8mm

Engine:
Spa 8T 105hp

Range:
200km (125 miles)

Speed:
32km/h (20mph)

Fording:
1m (3.25ft)

Trench Crossing:
2.1m (6.88ft)

Armour (hull):
6mm (.23in)

Armour (turret):
30mm (1.18in)

The first prototype of the M11/39 was built in 1937. It had a suspension system scaled up from that of the L3/35, a rear engine with drive sprockets at the front, a 37mm gun in the front right-hand side of the hull, a driver's compartment on the left, and a machine-gun turret on the hull roof.

Suspension for the tank consisted of two four-wheel bogie units each side. Each group of four wheels was in two pairs, controlled by a single semi-elliptic leaf spring. The powerplant was an excellent V-form eight-cylinder diesel engine, which produced a top speed of 32km/h (20mph). The hull gun was a semi-automatic weapon based on an old Vickers design, though it had only a limited traverse. Turret armament consisted of twin 8mm Breda machine guns in a two mounting.

Despite its mechanical reliability, the M11/39 was a poor fighting machine due to its ineffectual armament. This did not matter when the Italians were fighting poorly armed African troops, but against more modern armies it suffered badly.

It was used in Libya in 1940, though by this time it was obsolete. Many tanks were easily knocked out by British guns and the tank was swiftly withdrawn from service. A few captured vehicles were used by the Australians in North Africa in early 1941.

CARRO ARMATO M13/40

The M13/40 was a great improvement on the M11/39 due to its more powerful main gun and fully rotating turret. The prototype appeared in early 1940, and production was speeded up as Italy was about to enter the war. The first production vehicles rolled off the assembly line in July.

The lower hull was almost identical to that of the M11/39, although the engine was improved to give 125hp. The steering and final drive systems were also improved to give a more compact and efficient layout. The suspension system was strengthened to carry the greater weight of the vehicle by adding an extra leaf to the semi-elliptic springs.

The main armament consisted of the Ansaldo-built 47mm gun with a coaxial Breda 8mm machine gun in a hydraulically traversed turret. In addition, two Breda 38 machine guns were set in a twin mounting in the front right-hand side of the hull. Some models were further modified to take an up-rated Spa 15T engine which gave a higher speed.

The M13/40 was first used in action in North Africa in December 1940. Although inferior to comparable German tanks, it was at least equal to British cruiser tanks of the period and put up a very credible performance. A total of 1960 were built.

SPECIFICATIONS

CARRO ARMATO M13/40

Designation:
Carro Armato M13/40

Type:
Medium Tank

Length:
4.93m (16.18ft)

Width:
2.15m (7.08ft)

Height:
2.37m (7.8ft)

Weight:
14,254kg (31,360lb)

Crew:
Three

Main Armament:
47mm

Secondary Armament:
2 x 8mm

Engine:
Spa 15T 145hp

Range:
200km (125 miles)

Speed:
35.2km/h (22mph)

Fording:
1m (3.25ft)

Trench Crossing:
2.1m (6.88ft)

Armour (hull):
30mm (1.18in)

Armour (turret):
40mm (1.57in)

CARRO VELOCE 33

SPECIFICATIONS

CARRO VELOCE 33

Designation: **Carro Veloce 33**	Secondary Armament: **None**
Type: **Tankette**	Engine: **20hp**
Length: **3.16m (10.4ft)**	Range: **185km (115 miles)**
Width: **1.7m (5.6ft)**	Speed: **41.6km/h (26mph)**
Height: **1.29m (4.25ft)**	Fording: **.5m (1.64ft)**
Weight: **3207kg (7056lb)**	Trench Crossing: **1.4m (4.59ft)**
Crew: **Two**	Armour (hull): **15mm (.59in)**
Main Armament: **2 x 8mm**	Armour (superstructure): **5mm (.19in)**

Designed by Ansaldo, this vehicle closely resembled the Carro Veloce 29 tankette. The latter had been designed to accompany infantry and for general reconnaissance duties, and was in reality nothing more than a machine-gun carrier. The design of the 33 was finalised in 1933, and the Italian government, pleased with the design, placed an initial order for 1300 vehicles, which was later increased.

There were numerous variants and improved models, and it was widely used by the Italians and exported to a number of countries. Because of its light weight it could be carried by an aircraft, and on the ground could tow a tracked ammunition trailer. Its design was distinguished by being very low and small, and its lack of a turret meant the guns had to be set in the superstructure. The hull was of a rivetted and bolted construction, with the engine placed in the rear.

Other users of this vehicle included Afghanistan, Albania, Austria (illustrated above), Bolivia, Brazil, Bulgaria, China, Greece, Hungary, Iraq and Spain.

Variants included the 33/II, which had twin 8mm machine guns and improved vision ports, a version with a water-cooled machine gun. The L38 had stronger suspension, new tracks and some were fitted with a 20mm antitank gun.

L 35/LF

The basis of the L3/35 tankette was a Carden-Loyd Mk VI vehicle, 25 of which were purchased by the Italian Army in 1929. Based on these, a model known as the Carro Veloce ("fast tank") CV 28 was built by the Fiat motor works in conjunction with the Ansaldo armaments concern. This was followed by further models: CV 29 and CV L3/33. The Carro L3/35 was the final model.

The transmission was led forward to the clutch and gearbox, which had four forward speeds, in front of the driver, with final drive to front track sprockets. The fighting compartment was in the centre, with two crew members – driver on the right and gunner on the left – sitting side by side.

The L35/Lf was a flamethrower conversion of any of the three production types. Each vehicle towed a 500kg (1100lb) armoured fuel trailer, while the flame gun was mounted in the hull, replacing the machine guns. On some later vehicles the fuel tank was mounted on the rear superstructure. The range of the flame gun was approximately 100m (328ft). Though this vehicle was obsolete by 1929, it fought in North Africa in 1940–41 and some even saw service on the Eastern Front. Needless to say, for a vehicle that could be knocked out by the smallest antitank gun, they were easy prey for Red Army antitank gunners.

SPECIFICATIONS

L 35/LF

Designation:
Carro Armato L35/Lf

Type:
Flamethrower

Length:
3.16m (10.4ft)

Width:
1.7m (5.6ft)

Height:
1.29m (4.25ft)

Weight:
3207kg (7056lb)

Crew:
Two

Main Armament:
Flame Gun

Secondary Armament:
None

Engine:
20hp

Range:
150km (93.75 miles)

Speed:
41.6km/h (26mph)

Fording:
.5m (1.64ft)

Trench Crossing:
1.4m (4.59ft)

Armour (hull):
15mm (.59in)

Armour (turret):
5mm (.19in)

SEMOVENTE M40

SPECIFICATIONS

SEMOVENTE M40/41

Designation:
Semovente M40/41

Secondary Armament:
None

Type:
Self-propelled Gun

Engine:
140km (87.5 miles)

Length:
4.91m (16.1ft)

Range:
150km (93.75 miles)

Width:
2.28m (7.48ft)

Speed:
34km/h (21.25mph)

Height:
1.85m (6.06ft)

Fording:
1m (3.25ft)

Weight:
13,643kg (30,016lb)

Trench Crossing:
2.1m (6.88ft)

Crew:
Three

Armour (hull):
14mm (.55in)

Main Armament:
75mm

Armour (turret):
30mm (1.18in)

This self-propelled gun mounted the 75mm cannon, and as such it was a useful vehicle in tank-versus-tank actions. However, it proved woefully inadequate against T-34s and KV-1s on the Eastern Front.

The Italian presence on the Russian frontline was large in terms of men, but totally marginal in terms of armoured resources. The CSIR (Corpo di Spedizione Italiano in Russia), a 60,000-strong corps, and later the ARMIR (Armata Italiana in Russia), a 200,000-strong army, between them, and during the whole of their time in Russia, could muster only 55 L33/35 light tanks of the Gruppo Squadroni Carri Veloci "S.Giorgio" (a cavalry unit of the 3 Divisione Celere), 60 L6/40 light tanks of the 67th Battaglione Bersaglieri, and some 15 Semovente self-propelled guns.

The light tanks, being absolutely useless when it came to combat with other tanks, were used as support to infantry and mountain infantry units. All the tanks and the SP guns disappeared during the disastrous retreat in the southern sector of the Eastern Front in late 1942 and early 1943 following (more than 100,000 Italian soldiers died or were reported as missing in action) the fall of Stalingrad. The M40 did prove useful in North Africa against light British tanks, though, and was still being used in that theatre in early 1943.

SHI-KI

A variant of the Type 97 tank, the SHI-KI version served as a command vehicle for Japanese armoured regiments. It had the 37mm gun situated in the hull front in place of the machine gun. Another version mounted a 57mm gun duplicated in the hull front. The chief features of the tank were improvements in vision, communications and the incorporation of a directing device. The distinctive physical feature was the frame-type radio aerial around the turret.

Another variant of the Type 97 was a recovery vehicle. It was designed and equipped for rapid recovery of disabled vehicles and was built by Mitsubishi. The recovery equipment itself was simple: a rear light jib for lifting and steel ropes for towing. The tank's turret was conical-shaped. The mine-clearing version consisted of two revolving drums carrying rows of chains which exploded mines on contact. The main gun was retained in the turret.

The Type 97 had a bell-crank suspension with helical springs but no shock absorbers. The four centre wheels were mounted in pairs and operated against horizontally mounted compression springs, while the front and rear wheels acted on slopingly mounted compression springs. Drive was carried through a four-speed sliding gearbox combined with a high-and-low transfer case.

SPECIFICATIONS

COMMAND TANK SHI-KI

Designation:
Command Tank

Type:
Medium Tank

Length:
5.48m (18ft)

Width:
5.48m (18ft)

Height:
2.23m (7.33ft)

Weight:
15,272kg (33,600lb)

Crew:
Four

Main Armament:
37mm

Secondary Armament:
None

Engine:
Diesel V-12 170hp

Range:
230km (143.75 miles)

Speed:
37.6km/h (23.5mph)

Fording:
.8m (2.62ft)

Trench Crossing:
2.6m (8.53ft)

Armour (hull):
8mm (.31in)

Armour (turret):
25mm (.98in)

TYPE 94

SPECIFICATIONS

TYPE 94

Designation:
Tankette Type 94 TK

Type:
Tankette

Length:
3m (10ft)

Width:
1.62m (5.33ft)

Height:
1.62m (5.33ft)

Weight:
3563kg (7840lb)

Crew:
Two

Main Armament:
7.7mm

Secondary Armament:
None

Engine:
Four-cylinder petrol 32hp

Range:
160km (100 miles)

Speed:
40km/h (25mph)

Fording:
Unknown

Trench Crossing:
Unknown

Armour (hull):
4mm (.15in)

Armour (turret):
12mm (.47in)

The Type 94 was the result of a request from the Japanese Army in the early 1930s for an armoured tractor able to pull a tracked trailer for supplying ammunition to troops in the forward battle area. Its running gear consisted of four rubber-tyred bogie wheels each side, which were mounted on bell cranks resisted by compression springs. The turret was offset to the right, and traverse was achieved by shoulder pressure against the machine gun! A further problem was that when the driver's hatch was open, it interfered with the machine-gun traverse, thus the turret was often carried facing to the left.

The Japanese produced a modified version of the Type 94 from 1936 onwards, which incorporated a trailer idler, a lowered drive sprocket and an increased ground contact length for the tracks. The hull was made up of both welded and rivetted parts, and the interior of the driving and fighting compartments, plus the hull, were lined with asbestos panels to give protection against heat radiation.

A diesel version of the Type 94 was built as a prototype. The driver was situated to the left instead of to the right as in earlier variants. Though this tank never went into production, experience gained with it was used in the design of the Type 97 tankette.

TYPE 95

The Type 95 was the best Japanese tank of World War II. It was developed from 1933 to provide a vehicle with speed and mobility for the new mechanised brigades (though steel shortages and a lack of skilled labour meant many never materialized). It had a turret offset to the left, a prominent built-out front machine-gun compartment and two rounded bulges in the centre of the super-structure, which overhung the tracks. The hull and turret were composed of rivetted and bolted plates.

The Type 95 HA-GO had an air-cooled diesel engine that was of an advanced design, and it produced a high output in relation to its weight. Power drive was transmitted to the front sprockets through a sliding gearbox giving four forward gears and one reverse.

There was a modified version of the Type 95, which had a specialized track to improve cross-country performance. The wheels were coupled in pairs by low-attached bogie bolsters of inverted triangular shape. This modification was intended for tanks deployed to the Manchuria theatre.

The Type 98 was a further development of the HA-GO, and ran on six wheels grouped a three bogies each side, with their springing system located inside. Tracks remained front driven, and there was neither hull nor turret rear machine gun, and no cupola above the turret.

SPECIFICATIONS

TYPE 95

Designation: **Light Tank Type 95**	Secondary Armament: **2 x 7.7mm**
Type: **Light Tank**	Engine: **Diesel Six-cylinder**
Length: **4.1m (13.46ft)**	Range: **250km (156 miles)**
Width: **2.05m (6.72ft)**	Speed: **40km/h (25mph)**
Height: **2.28m (7.5ft)**	Fording: **1m (3.25ft)**
Weight: **7534kg (16,576lb)**	Trench Crossing: **2m (6.56ft)**
Crew: **Three**	Armour (hull): **6mm (.23in)**
Main Armament: **37mm**	Armour (turret): **14mm (.55in)**

TYPE 97

SPECIFICATIONS

TYPE 97

Designation:
Medium Tank Type 97

Type:
Medium Tank

Length:
5.5m (18.04ft)

Width:
2.33m (7.64ft)

Height:
2.38m (7.8ft)

Weight:
16,087kg (35,392lb)

Crew:
Four

Main Armament:
57mm

Secondary Armament:
1 x 7.7mm

Engine:
Mitsubishi V-12

Range:
210km (131.25 miles)

Speed:
38km/h (23.75mph)

Fording:
1m (3.25ft)

Trench Crossing:
2m (6.5ft)

Armour (hull):
6mm (.23in)

Armour (turret):
33mm (1.29in)

Introduced in 1937, the medium tank Type 97, CHI-HA, was one of the best Japanese tanks of World War II, though it was not a match for any US or British main battle tank. The design drew upon European designs, especially Axis, and improvements over other Japanese tanks included a new suspension system. However, as there were still no shock absorbers the tank was a rough ride for the crew. From 1942 onwards the tank underwent a number of changes, including a larger turret mounting a 47mm high-velocity gun. This model was known as the Shinhoto CHI-HA, and production continued until the end of the war.

Japanese tank divisions had two tank brigades, each one equipped with two tank regiments. These were at the heart of the division. There was also a mechanized infantry regiment, though the troops were carried in trucks not halftracks. Other divisional units included a mechanized artillery regiment, antitank battalion, antiaircraft defence unit, a tank reconnaissance unit, a divisional engineer unit, a divisional maintenance unit, a signals transport unit, and a transport unit. Most armoured divisions were stationed in Manchuria and China, such as the 1st Tank Division, first formed as a tank group in December 1941. It ended the war stationed in Japan itself.

LIGHT TANK 7TP

The Polish 7TP began as a development of the Vickers-Armstrong Mk E tank, a number of which were purchased from Great Britain between 1932 and 1934. These tanks appeared in two versions: one with two turrets armed with two machine guns and the other with a single machine gun.

The 7TP was also produced in two versions at first, but later versions were built only as the single-turret variant. The final model was produced until 1939. The final variant had a Vickers suspension and had a special Polish turret (built in Sweden) with a 37mm main gun and coaxial machine gun. A Saurer-designed diesel engine was used in the Polish tank in place of the petrol model used in the earlier Vickers tanks, which helped to maintain a similar performance to that of earlier tanks, although the armour was increased to a maximum of 40mm (1.57in)

Around 170 7TPs of all types were built, and they formed the backbone of Polish armoured formations in September 1939. Although they were outdated when compared to the German panzers, they were in fact better armed than the Panzer Is and IIs which at the time formed the bulk of German armoured strength. The problem was that the Polish Army just did not have enough to defeat the panzers.

SPECIFICATIONS

LIGHT TANK 7TP

Designation: **Light Tank 7TP**	Secondary Armament: **1 x 7.92mm**
Type: **Light Tank**	Engine: **Saurer Diesel Six-cylinder**
Length: **4.57m (15ft)**	Range: **160km (100 miles)**
Width: **2.43m (8ft)**	Speed: **32km/h (20mph)**
Height: **2.13m (7ft)**	Fording: **Unknown**
Weight: **9571kg (21,056lb)**	Trench Crossing: **3.12m (10.23ft)**
Crew: **Three**	Armour (hull): **15mm (.59in)**
Main Armament: **37mm**	Armour (turret): **40mm (1.57in)**

COMBAT CAR M1

SPECIFICATIONS

COMBAT CAR M1

Designation: **Combat Car M1**	Secondary Armament: **None**
Type: **Light Tank**	Engine: **Guiberson 250hp**
Length: **4.45m (14.6ft)**	Range: **112km (70 miles)**
Width: **2.69m (7.75ft)**	Speed: **72km/h (45mph)**
Height: **2.36m (7.75ft)**	Fording: **.9m (3ft)**
Weight: **8877kg (19,530lb)**	Trench Crossing: **1.83m (6ft)**
Crew: **Four**	Armour (hull): **12.7m (.5in)**
Main Armament: **4 x .5in**	Armour (turret): **19mm (.75in)**

Produced at the Rock Island Arsenal in 1937, the Combat Car M1 was a development of the Combat Car T1 design for US cavalry units. The Combat Car was in fact a tank built for the cavalry scouting role, but the nomenclature was necessary to bypass the law of Congress of 1920 which made tanks the sole province of the infantry. Individuals such as J. Walter Christie had carried out independent tank development, and his ideas for fast, light tanks with powerful engines and effective suspension would have a profound effect on American tank development.

There were a number of versions of the M1. The M1E2, for example, had a modified engine space and rear bogie moved back some 280mm (11in). The rear of the hull was reshaped for better access and to increase fuel capacity. The Combat Car M1E3 was the M1 fitted with experimental continuous band rubber tracks, and later with rubber tracks. It was built in 1939, but only for trials purposes.

The Combat Car M2 was like the Combat Car M1A1 (which was fitted with constant mesh transmission, turret offset to the right and a radio), but with improved turret and fixed with a Guiberson T1020 diesel engine. A trailing idler was also introduced on this model. The vehicle was redesignated Light Tank M1A1 in 1940.

HEAVY TANK M6

The US Army had considered the need for a heavy tank in 1939, and so the development of the T1 was approved in May 1940. Approval was given to build four variants in February 1941 to test alternative forms of transmission and hull forms. These models were the T1E1, with cast hull and electric drive; T1E2, with cast hull and torque converter drive; T1E3, with welded hull and torque converter drive; and T1E4 with welded hull, four diesel engines and twin Torquematic transmission.

The end result of trials was that the T1E2 was standardised during May 1942 as the Heavy Tank M6, while the T1E3 was standardised as the Heavy Tank M6A1. The only external difference between the two was the welded hull of the latter.

It was planned to produce 5500 M6s, but this was reduced in September 1942 to 115. The US Armored Force had meanwhile been testing the vehicle and found the M6 to be too heavy, undergunned, poorly shaped and having a faulty transmission. Because of these problems and tactical limitations, there was little need for this type of vehicle. As a result, only 40 M6s were built, and these consisted of eight M6s, 12 M6A1s and 20 M6A2s. The series was declared obsolete in late 1944. The US tank that eventually became the answer to the German Panthers and Tigers was the Pershing.

SPECIFICATIONS

HEAVY TANK M6

Designation: **Heavy Tank M6**	Secondary Armament: **4 x .5in**
Type: **Heavy Tank**	Engine: **Wright G-200 800hp**
Length: **7.54m (24.75ft)**	Range: **Unknown**
Width: **3.09m (10.16ft)**	Speed: **35.2km/h (22mph)**
Height: **2.98m (9.8ft)**	Fording: **1.01m (3.3ft)**
Weight: **57,500kg (126,500lb)**	Trench Crossing: **3.04m (10ft)**
Crew: **Six**	Armour (hull): **25.4mm (1in)**
Main Armament: **1 x 3in, 1 x 37mm**	Armour (turret): **82.55mm (3.25in)**

LIGHT TANK M2A2

SPECIFICATIONS

LIGHT TANK M2A2

Designation: **Light Tank M2A2**	Secondary Armament: **2 x .3in**
Type: **Light Tank**	Engine: **Continental Radial 250hp**
Length: **4.14m (13.6ft)**	Range: **100km (62.5 miles)**
Width: **2.38m (7.83ft)**	Speed: **72km/h (45mph)**
Height: **2.36m (7.75ft)**	Fording: **1m (3.28ft)**
Weight: **8681kg (19,100lb)**	Trench Crossing: **1.83m (6ft)**
Crew: **Four**	Armour (hull): **12.7mm (.5in)**
Main Armament: **.5in**	Armour (turret): **19mm (.75in)**

Design of the Light Tank T2 was started in 1933, and the pilot model appeared at the Rock Island Arsenal a year later. It was armed with two .3in machine guns, one .5in machine gun and powered by a Continental aircraft engine rated at 260hp. The M2A2 was developed from the T2, being armed like the T2.

The Browning .3in machine gun was designed in 1919 and was a very reliable weapon. It was the standard US tank machine gun throughout World War II. A major advantage was the small hole required in a tank's armour for fitment, though the fabric of its ammunition belt was poor and the feed was not interchangeable between left and right. It had a muzzle velocity of 823m/sec (2700ft/sec) and could fire ball or armour-piercing ammunition.

The Browning .5in was a scaled-up version of the .3in version, and was used primarily in the antiaircraft role. However, it was also used as the main armament of the M2 Combat Car. As well as being the standard antiaircraft machine gun for most US tanks, it served the same purpose on many British tanks.

The M2A2E2 was an M2A2 with modified suspension and thicker armour, while the M2A2E3, which was developed in 1938, had a modified suspension with trailing idler and had a GM diesel engine.

LIGHT TANK M2A4

The M2A4 was one of a line of tanks developed from 1933 onwards and was the first to carry the 37mm gun. This gun was the standard weapon of US light and medium tanks in the period immediately prior to World War II. The M2A4 also had the distinction of being one of the earliest types of fighting vehicle to be supplied to Britain in 1941.

The tank was powered by a Continental aircraft engine which gave a top speed of 59.2km/h (37mph). Its secondary armament, in addition to the turret coaxial .3in Browning, included two further Brownings in sponsons at either side of the driver's and co-driver's positions and another in the glacis plate. Suspension consisted of two two-wheeled bogie units each side, each unit sprung on vertical volute springs. The idler wheel was at the rear, off the ground, and the drive sprocket at the front.

A total of 365 M2A4s was built, and a few of those fought with US forces in the Pacific theatre in 1942 during the early campaigns against the Japanese (the above photograph shows one such vehicle). Those delivered to Great Britain in 1941 – some 40 – were used for Home Defence and training, in which role they were used for familiarizing troops with the similar M3 Light Tank. As such, they provided a crucial service.

SPECIFICATIONS

LIGHT TANK M2A4

Designation:
Light Tank M2A4

Secondary Armament:
1 x .5in, 4 x .3in

Type:
Light Tank

Engine:
Continental Radial 250hp

Length:
4.14m (13.6ft)

Range:
128km (80 miles)

Width:
2.52m (8.3ft)

Speed:
59.2km/h (37mph)

Height:
2.36m (7.75in)

Fording:
1m (3.28ft)

Weight:
8681kg (19,100lb)

Trench Crossing:
1.83m (6ft)

Crew:
Four

Armour (hull):
12.7mm (.5in)

Main Armament:
37mm

Armour (turret):
19mm (.75in)

LIGHT TANK M3

SPECIFICATIONS

LIGHT TANK M3

Designation: **Light Tank M3**	Secondary Armament: **3 x .3in**
Type: **Light Tank**	Engine: **Continental Radial 250hp**
Length: **3.29m (14.8ft)**	Range: **112.6km (70 miles)**
Width: **2.24m (7.34ft)**	Speed: **56km/h (35mph)**
Height: **2.51m (8.25ft)**	Fording: **.9m (3ft)**
Weight: **12,523kg (27,552lb)**	Trench Crossing: **1.83m (6ft)**
Crew: **Four**	Armour (hull): **25.4mm (1in)**
Main Armament: **37mm**	Armour (turret): **38.1mm (1.5in)**

Developed from the M2A4, the M3 incorporated improvements found to be necessary from experience with the earlier vehicle. The main change was the introduction of a large trailing idler wheel in place of the idler of the M2A4. This refinement helped to improve stability. As the M3 Stuart came after the outbreak of war, it was able to benefit from information gleaned from combat experience.

Armament remained the same as the M2A4, but it had thicker armour on the front plate and reinforced suspension to take the greater weight. Its hull was welded rather than riveted, and from mid-1941 a gyro-stabilization system was introduced for the main gun, while external fuel tanks were added for additional range.

The M3 entered production in March 1941, and some of the first production models were in the hands of British tank units in the Middle East by August of the same year. The M3 was called Stuart I by the British War Office, and was classed as a light cruiser tank by virtue of its armament and armour. The armament of the M3A1 consisted of a 37mm gun and three .3in Brownings, one coaxial with the main gun, one in the hull front and one as an antiaircraft gun on the turret roof. A variant of the M3 was the T2 mine exploder.

MEDIUM TANK T3

This tank began life as a development of the Christie M1928, a turretless vehicle designed by Christie and built in 1928 by the US Wheel and Track Layer Corporation. The main feature of the vehicle was its ability to run on wheels or tracks by means of the Christie suspension. This consisted of four large weight-carrying wheels on each side, mounted on arms connected to long adjustable springs housed vertically inside the side of the hull. Two of the tanks were sold to the USSR, where they became the basis for the BT series of tanks (see pages 85–87).

The Medium Tank T3 was produced by the same company in 1931, and was accepted into the US Army under the designation T3 Medium Tank. Fitted with a 37mm gun and coaxial .3in machine gun in a fully traversing turret, the original nose gun was eliminated. Four were delivered to the US Cavalry and were redesignated Combat Car T1.

The Medium Tank T3E1 was the designation of two machines contracted by the Polish government, though they eventually entered the US Army as the Poles defaulted on payment. They were similar to the US version, but had a gear drive when operating as wheeled vehicles. The Medium Tank T3E2 had a sloped, widened nose and enlarged turret.

SPECIFICATIONS

MEDIUM TANK T3

Designation: **Medium Tank T3**	Secondary Armament: **1 x .3in**
Type: **Medium Tank**	Engine: **Liberty V-12 338hp**
Length: **5.49m (18ft)**	Range: **Unknown**
Width: **2.41m (7.3ft)**	Speed: **110.4km/h (69mph)**
Height: **2.29m (7.5ft)**	Fording: **1m (3.28ft)**
Weight: **11,200kg (24,640lb)**	Trench Crossing: **2.1m (10.7ft)**
Crew: **Three**	Armour (hull): **6mm (.23in)**
Main Armament: **37mm**	Armour (turret): **13mm (.51in)**

M22 LOCUST

SPECIFICATIONS

M22 LOCUST

Designation:
Light Tank T9E1

Type:
Light Tank

Length:
3.93m (12.9ft)

Width:
2.2m (7.25ft)

Height:
1.72m (5.66ft)

Weight:
7454kg (16,400lb)

Crew:
Three

Main Armament:
37mm

Secondary Armament:
1 x .3in

Engine:
Lycoming 162hp

Range:
224km (140 miles)

Speed:
56km/h (35mph)

Fording:
.9m (3ft)

Trench Crossing:
1.52m (5ft)

Armour (hull):
19.05mm (.75in)

Armour (turret):
25.4mm (1in)

In February 1941 the US Army had expressed a requirement for an air-portable tank. Design studies were submitted by General Motors Corp., the Marmon-Herrington Co. and J. Walter Christie. The Marmon-Herrington design, which employed the Lycoming six-cylinder air-cooled engine and Marmon-Herrington suspension and tracks, was accepted.

The first test model was delivered in the autumn of 1941. The vehicle itself was satisfactory, but there was room for further improvement, and so further design studies of an improved vehicle, the T9E1, were begun in February 1942. These involved the reshaping of the front hull, eliminating the bow machine gun, and removing the turret traverse and gyrostabilizer to decrease weight. The turret and turret basket were removable for air transportation.

The first production models rolled off the production line in March 1943, and some 830 were built between then and February 1944. However, it was never used in action by the US Army, chiefly because the latter lacked an aircraft or glider to transport it. The M22 was supplied to the British, who had the Hamilcar glider to transport it, and it became known as the Locust. It was used by the 6th Airborne Division during the spectacular Rhine crossing in March 1945.

M24 CHAFFEE

Development of the Light Tank T24 began in April 1943 to provide the US Army with an improved vehicle with greater mobility, flotation and accessibility, and also armed with a larger gun than the 37mm weapon used by its predecessors. The first pilot was delivered in October 1943, and following successful trials an order was placed for 5000 vehicles, become the M24 Chaffee in service.

Though it employed the Cadillac powerplant and Hydra-Matic transmission of the M5 series of tanks, it was a redesigned vehicle. The M24 was a low-sleek vehicle with well-sloped armour and large-diameter road wheels sprung on traverse torsion bars. Its main armament was a turret-mounted lightweight 75mm M6 (L/39) gun developed from an aircraft weapon, which employed a space-saving concentric recoil mechanism. It was stabilized in elevation, and the turret had hydraulic power and manual traverse.

The Chaffee was built by two manufacturers – Cadillac and Massey Harris – and by the end of the war a total of 4070 vehicles had been produced in total (a small number being supplied to the British). Used in Europe and the Pacific, the M24 proved itself a good reconnaissance tank with excellent manoeuvrability, which could hold its own in a firefight with the enemy.

SPECIFICATIONS

M24 CHAFFEE

Designation:
Light Tank M24

Type:
Light Tank

Length:
5.48m (18ft)

Width:
2.95m (9.67ft)

Height:
2.46m (8.1ft)

Weight:
18,409kg (40,500lb)

Crew:
Five

Main Armament:
75mm

Secondary Armament:
2 x .3in, 1 x .5in

Engine:
2 x Cadillac 110hp

Range:
160km (100 miles)

Speed:
56km/h (35mph)

Fording:
1.02m (3.34ft)

Trench Crossing:
2.44m (8ft)

Armour (hull):
28mm (1.1in)

Armour (turret):
38mm (1.49in)

M26 PERSHING

SPECIFICATIONS

M26 PERSHING

Designation:
Heavy Tank T26E3

Type:
Heavy Tank

Length:
6.32m (20.75ft)

Width:
3.5m (11.5ft)

Height:
2.77m (9.1ft)

Weight:
41,818kg (92,000lb)

Crew:
Five

Main Armament:
90mm

Secondary Armament:
2 x .3in, 1 x .5in

Engine:
Ford GAF V-8

Range:
160km (100 miles)

Speed:
32km/h (20mph)

Fording:
1.21m (4ft)

Trench Crossing:
2.28m (7.48ft)

Armour (hull):
50.8mm (2in)

Armour (turret):
101.6mm (4in)

The US Army came to appreciate the need for a heavy tank very late in the war, and it was only in November 1944 that the first 20 prototypes were built. The German Ardennes Offensive of December 1944, during which the inadequacies of the M4 Sherman were revealed once again, prompted the US General Staff to order the immediate despatch of the T26 heavy tank to Europe. The first 20 arrived in January 1945 and were issued to combat units.

The tank's main armament was the 90mm Tank Gun M3. With a muzzle velocity of 1021m/sec (3350ft/sec), it still did not match the German 75mm or 88mm guns that armed the Panthers and Tigers. That said, it had a reasonable performance against enemy armour when firing the armour-piercing, composite rigid round, and its high-explosive round was excellent. The gun was mounted in a turret that had a 360-degree traverse, and the crew consisted of a commander, driver, co-driver, gunner and loader.

Crews found the General Pershing a good fighting vehicle: it was almost a match for the fearsome German Tiger in terms of firepower, and surpassed it with regard to mobility and reliability. A few were sent to Great Britain for trails, but the end of the war in Europe limited the numbers sent.

MEDIUM TANK M3

The M3 was the result of a meeting between the Chief of the Armored Forces and the Ordnance Department. The desire was for the 75mm gun to be mounted in a turret, but insufficient development work had been done on the problem of mounting a large-calibre gun in a revolving turret. However, as experiments had already been carried out on mounting a 75mm pack howitzer in a modified sponson, it was decided that the 75mm gun would be mounted in the right sponson of the new vehicle.

The new vehicle was called the Medium Tank M3, and it had the same Wright radial engine as the M2A1. Its turret and sponson were cast while the rest of hull was riveted, though changes were made in later models. The most important features were the gyrostabilizers for the 75mm and 37mm guns, which meant they could be fired accurately while the vehicle was moving. The A1 version had a cast upper hull, while the A1E1 version was used as a test bed with triple six-cylinder Lycoming engines. The A2 model had an all-welded hull, and the A3 version was fitted with twin General Motors 6-71 diesel engines; the A4 was powered by a Chrysler A-57 Multibank engine; and the A5 was as the M3A3 but had a riveted hull. In all 4924 M3s were built by the time production ceased in August 1942.

SPECIFICATIONS

MEDIUM TANK M3

Designation: **Medium Tank M3**	Secondary Armament: **1 x 37mm, 3 x .3in**
Type: **Medium Tank**	Engine: **Wright Continental 340hp**
Length: **5.63m (18.5ft)**	Range: **193km (120 miles)**
Width: **2.72m (8.92ft)**	Speed: **41.6km/h (26mph)**
Height: **3.12m (10.25ft)**	Fording: **1.02m (3.3ft)**
Weight: **27,272kg (30,000lb)**	Trench Crossing: **1.91m (6. 25ft)**
Crew: **Six**	Armour (hull): **38.1mm (1.5in)**
Main Armament: **75mm**	Armour (turret): **50.8mm (2in)**

MEDIUM TANK M4A1

SPECIFICATIONS

MEDIUM TANK M4A1

Designation:
Medium Tank M4A1

Type:
Medium Tank

Length:
5.83m (19.16ft)

Width:
2.6m (8.53ft)

Height:
2.74m (9ft)

Weight:
30,227kg (66,500lb)

Crew:
Five

Main Armament:
75mm

Secondary Armament:
2 x .3in, 1 x .5in

Engine:
Continental 400hp

Range:
160km (100 miles)

Speed:
38.4km/h (24mph)

Fording:
.9m (3ft)

Trench Crossing:
2.26m (7.41ft)

Armour (hull):
25.4mm (1in)

Armour (turret):
50.8mm (2in)

Of the tanks that saw service in World War II, the M4 Sherman was probably the most important, and certainly most widely produced, of all tanks to see service with the Allies in the war. In 1941 it was decided to use the M3 lower hull, powerplant, transmission and running gear for a new tank, with a redesigned upper hull mounting a central turret armed with a 75mm gun. A prototype was completed in September 1941, and initial production was placed at 2000 per month. The first models saw combat at El Alamein in October 1942, and from then on it became the backbone of Allied armoured strength. In all, over 40,000 were built.

The Sherman was reliable, easy to maintain, rugged and highly mobile. Though it lacked the firepower of German and Soviet tanks, it was up-gunned and up-armoured throughout its life. The A1, standardised in December 1941, had a cast hull designed to present less flat surfaces to a direct hit from any angle. It also had a three-piece differential housing and vision slots in the front armour. Later production models of the A1 had periscopes replacing the vision slots for the driver and appliqué armour attached to the turret.

The Sherman continued to serve as a frontline tank after World War II: the Israelis used them to great effect in their early conflicts in the Middle East.

MEDIUM TANK M4A3

Having a welded hull and cast turret, the A3 was powered by a 500hp Ford engine. The early production model was equipped with the M34 gun mount, vision slots in the front armour and a cast, one-piece round-nosed differential housing. The vision slots were replaced on later models by periscopes for the driver, and this model was also fitted with sand shields. The last version of the A3 was equipped with the 75mm gun in an M34A1 gun mount, a vision cupola for the tank commander, and placed a small oval hatch over the loader's position.

Other features of this vehicle included a 47-degree front armour plate on the hull, larger driver's doors and a cast one-piece, sharp-nosed differential housing. Some versions were fitted with 75mm ammunition racks which had liquid-filled containers on either side to prevent fire in case the side of the vehicle was pierced. As this arrangement was known as "wet stowage", models fitted with this feature were known as M4A3W.

The first up-gunning of the Sherman involved replacing the 75mm gun with the 76mm model, which was a high-velocity weapon designed to knock out all enemy tanks then in service. Unfortunately, its antitank performance was inferior to the guns mounted by German Tiger and Panther tanks.

SPECIFICATIONS

MEDIUM TANK M4A3

Designation:
Medium Tank M4A3

Type:
Medium Tank

Length:
6m (19.66ft)

Width:
2.6m (8.53ft)

Height:
2.74m (9ft)

Weight:
31,136kg (68,500lb)

Crew:
Five

Main Armament:
75mm

Secondary Armament:
2 x .3in, 1 x .5in

Engine:
Ford GAA-III 500hp

Range:
160km (100 miles)

Speed:
40km/h (25mph)

Fording:
.9m (3ft)

Trench Crossing:
2.26m (7.41ft)

Armour (hull):
25.4mm (1in)

Armour (turret):
50.8mm (2in)

MINE EXPLODER T3

SPECIFICATIONS

MINE EXPLODER T3

Designation:
Mine Exploder T3

Type:
Anti-mine Tank

Length:
8.23m (27ft)

Width:
3.5m (11.48ft)

Height:
2.74m (9ft)

Weight:
31,818kg (70,000lb)

Crew:
Five

Main Armament:
75mm

Secondary Armament:
2 x .3in. 1 x .5in

Engine:
Ford GAA V-8 500hp

Range:
62km (100 miles)

Speed:
46km/h (28.75mph)

Fording:
.9m (3ft)

Trench Crossing:
2.26m (7.5ft)

Armour (hull):
25.4mm (1in)

Armour (turret):
76mm (2.99in)

The problem of having to deal with enemy mines, especially when having to breach heavily defended Axis positions, resulted in a number of special variants of the Sherman fitted with rollers, flails and plunger rods. The Mine Exploder T1 was developed in 1943 and put into limited production. It consisted of two roller units, each of five 3m- (10ft-) diameter steel discs driven by a roller chain from the tank's drive sprocket.

The Mine Exploder T1E4 was developed as a more manoeuvrable version, and consisted of 16 discs, each of 1219mm (48in) diameter, mounted in a single heavy frame unit which was driven in front of the tank.

The T3 was developed in 1943 and based on the British Scorpion flail device, which had proved to be a success and relatively simple to manufacture. It consisted of two booms extending forward from the tank with a rotating shaft fitted with chains to beat the ground as the tank advanced. Power for the rotor was obtained from an auxiliary engine.

The T8 was a curious vehicle, having a series of vertical plunger rods mounted on a pivoted frame in front of the tank. It was geared to strike the ground as the tank moved forward, and thus detonate any mines in its path. The device was tested in 1944, but only one pilot model was built.

SHERMAN FLAMETHROWER

Flamethrowers have traditionally exerted a powerful psychological effect on opponents. It was therefore logical that the Americans should develop a flamethrower version of their main battle tank. In fact, the US Army developed a number of flamethrower tanks. The M4-3 was a standard Sherman that could be fitted with a flamethrower kit that was installed in place of the bow machine gun, with a 22-gallon fuel tank situated in the right sponson.

The POA-CWS 75-HI Flamethrower was a Pacific theatre improvisation. It used a US Navy Mk I flamethrower with the projector tube fitted inside the barrel of a 75mm M3 gun. Some 62 vehicles were thus converted, and found much work in incinerating stubborn Japanese defenders during the Pacific War.

The Anti-Personnel Tank Projector E1 was developed in 1945, and consisted of four special flamethrowers that were mounted externally on Shermans to protect them from enemy troops attempting to place bombs or magnetic mines on the vehicles. Each unit was controlled electrically from within the vehicle by a push-button switch. They could be fired singly or simultaneously. The final flamethrower Sherman was the T33, which carried the flame fuel and propellant gas inside the vehicle.

SPECIFICATIONS

FLAMETHROWER

Designation:
Flamethrower Tank

Type:
Medium Tank

Length:
6m (19.66ft)

Width:
2.6m (8.53ft)

Height:
2.74m (9ft)

Weight:
31,136kg (68,500lb)

Crew:
Five

Main Armament:
75mm

Secondary Armament:
2 x .3in, 1 x .5in

Engine:
Ford GAA-III 500hp

Range:
160km (100 miles)

Speed:
40km/h (25mph)

Fording:
.9m (3ft)

Trench Crossing:
2.26m (7.41ft)

Armour (hull):
25.4mm (1in)

Armour (turret):
50.8mm (2in)

TANK DESTROYER M10

SPECIFICATIONS

TANK DESTROYER M10

Designation:
Gun Motor Carriage M10

Type:
Tank Destroyer

Length:
6.83m (22.5ft)

Width:
3.05m (10ft)

Height:
2.57m (8.4ft)

Weight:
29,937kg (65,861lb)

Crew:
Five

Main Armament:
76mm

Secondary Armament:
1 x .5in

Engine:
General Motors 375hp x 2

Range:
322km (200 miles)

Speed:
51km/h (32mph)

Fording:
.9m (3ft)

Trench Crossing:
2.26m (7.5ft)

Armour (hull):
12mm (.47in)

Armour (turret):
37mm (1.46in)

Before World War II, the US Army had devoted a great deal of thought to defeating large, fast-moving enemy tank formations. The answer it formulated was the employment of large numbers of tank destroyers. The Gun Motor Carriage M10 was the product of this concept. It was based on the M4A3 chassis and mounted the 76mm M7 (L/52) gun in a low, open-topped turret that had a 360-degree traverse. The five-man crew consisted of commander, driver and the three servers of the gun.

Production of the M10 began in September 1942 and had finished by December of the same year. By then some 7000 vehicles had been produced. In the field the concept of separate tank-destroyer battalions proved ineffective, and thus most M10s were used for offensive purposes to support attacks. The M10 continued in service until the end of the war, but by then had become obsolete. A few entered British service, being designated "3in SP Wolverine".

The M36 was a development of the M10, being armed with a 90mm gun in place of the smaller weapon in a larger turret. This vehicle was an excellent tank destroyer, and true to the original US Army concept, and could take on the Tigers and Panthers of the enemy on an equal footing.

BT-2

In December 1930, the Soviet Union purchased two US Christie M1928 convertible tanks (see page 75), which became known in Soviet service as the BT-1. The first Soviet prototypes, known as the BT-2, were completed in October 1931 and took part in the Moscow parade on 7 November of that year.

The BT series of medium tanks were designed as fast vehicles undertaking the traditional cavalry role of exploitation. Production of the BT-2 began in 1932 and was ended the following year, by which time 4000 vehicles had been built. The tank was fast, but was unreliable and was cramped for the three-man crew. The tank did have some interesting features, such as the capability of running either on its tracks or on its road wheels as required. Armament was satisfactory for its intended role, with a 37mm main gun and a ball-mounted machine gun. Amazingly, this tank was still in service in 1940.

The BT-3 was a modified version of the BT-2, with solid disc wheels in place of the spoked type of earlier vehicles. It was also up-gunned with a 45mm gun. The BT-4 was a prototype with hull features similar to the BT-3 but with twin turrets replacing the single turret. The major problem with the BT-2 was its mechanical unreliability, a problem never entirely solved.

SPECIFICATIONS

BT-2

Designation:
BT-2

Type:
Medium Tank

Length:
5.48m (18ft)

Width:
2.23m (7.33ft)

Height:
1.92m (6.33ft)

Weight:
11,200kg (24,640lb)

Crew:
Three

Main Armament:
37mm

Secondary Armament:
1 x 7.62mm

Engine:
400hp

Range:
300km (187 miles)

Speed:
72km/h (45mph)

Fording:
1m (3.28ft)

Trench Crossing:
2.1m (10.7ft)

Armour (hull):
6mm (.23in)

Armour (turret):
13mm (.51in)

BT-5

SPECIFICATIONS

BT-5

Designation:
BT-5

Type:
Medium Tank

Length:
5.48m (18ft)

Width:
2.23m (7.33ft)

Height:
2.2m (7.25ft)

Weight:
11,709kg (25,760lb)

Crew:
Three

Main Armament:
45mm

Secondary Armament:
1 x 7.62mm

Engine:
Type M5 350hp

Range:
200km (125 miles)

Speed:
70km/h (43.75mph)

Fording:
1m (3.28ft)

Trench Crossing:
1m (3.28ft)

Armour (hull):
6mm (.23in)

Armour (turret):
13mm (.51in)

Problems with the BT-2 came to a head during the November 1932 Moscow parade, when two of the vehicles broke down during the display (the comments of the watching Soviet leaders are not recorded!). This prompted two new designs intended to improve the tank's reliability and battlefield potency – the BT-3 and BT-4 – but they were both rejected. The BT-5 was a major production model with an enlarged cylindrical turret, 45mm main gun, a new engine, improved vision devices and a stronger suspension.

The 45mm Tank Gun M32 was an excellent weapon for its time. With a muzzle velocity of 760m/sec (2492ft/sec), it had good armour penetration. However, as tank armour increased in thickness it became outclassed and was eventually replaced in Soviet tanks by the 76.2mm gun.

The BT-5(V) was a commander's tank. It was identical to the BT-5 apart from a frame round the turret and the provision of a radio in the rear turret overhang. The BT-5A was an artillery version of the tank, and mounted the 76.2mm Model 27/32 howitzer in the T-28 turret. Around 65 BT-5s fought in the Spanish Civil War, and they showed themselves to be superior to the German Panzer I and the Italian tankettes in service with the Nationalist forces.

BT-7

Though the BT-7 was superior to earlier models with regard to engine power, armour and armament, the BT-7 retained the qualities of high speed and good cross-country running ability. These were possible due to the excellent power-to-weight ratio and the Christie suspension, which consisted of four large-diameter road wheels each side, independently mounted at the end of leading or trailing swing arms, controlled by long coil springs. The springs were mounted between the inner and outer hull side plates.

When the tracks were removed (a process that took about an hour), the drive was transferred from the rear sprockets to the rear road wheels on each side. In this configuration the two front road wheels were used for steering instead of the clutch and brake system used when travelling on tracks.

Later BT-7s were armed with a 45mm gun and a coaxial 7.62mm machine gun, with sometimes a second machine gun mounted in the rear of the turret (which was mainly of welded construction).

The BT-7 was still in service in large numbers at the time of the German invasion of the Soviet Union in June 1941, but by then they were too lightly armoured to withstand the panzers, and were replaced as soon as possible by the T-34.

SPECIFICATIONS

BT-7

Designation:
BT-7

Type:
Medium Tank

Length:
5.68m (18.65ft)

Width:
2.43m (7.98ft)

Height:
2.28m (7.5ft)

Weight:
14,050kg (30,912lb)

Crew:
Three

Main Armament:
45mm

Secondary Armament:
2 x 7.62mm

Engine:
450hp

Range:
250km (156.25 miles)

Speed:
86km/h (53.75mph)

Fording:
1.56m (5.1ft)

Trench Crossing:
2.1m (10.7ft)

Armour (hull):
6mm (.23in)

Armour (turret):
22mm (.86in)

IS-2 JOSEPH STALIN

SPECIFICATIONS

IS-2 JOSEPH STALIN

Designation:
IS-2

Type:
Heavy Tank

Length:
8.32m (27.3ft)

Width:
3.09m (10.13ft)

Height:
2.73m (8.9ft)

Weight:
46,000kg (101,200lb)

Crew:
Four

Main Armament:
122mm

Secondary Armament:
4 x 7.62mm

Engine:
V-2-IS V-12 diesel 600hp

Range:
240km (149 miles)

Speed:
37km/h (23mph)

Fording:
Unknown

Trench Crossing:
2.49m (8.16ft)

Armour (hull):
120mm (4.72in)

Armour (turret):
132mm (5.19in)

The Josef Stalin series of heavy tanks was a development of the basic KV heavy tank, which the Red Army had wanted to give it superiority over the best German tanks then in service. The same engine was used as in the KV series, but with a synchromesh transmission and regenerative steering to simplify driving and increase manoeuvrability. The idlers, sprockets and return rollers of the chassis were lowered to allow the superstructure to overhang the tracks and thus accommodate the larger turret. Hull shape was improved to increase protection, and the tank mounted the 85mm tank gun in a three-man turret. This version was known as the IS-1A, but was soon replaced by the IS-1B which mounted the 100mm gun.

In early 1944 the IS-2 appeared, which was armed with the 122mm gun. The armour-piercing round it fired could penetrate 185mm (7.5in) of armour at 1000m (3280ft). However, because of the size of the weapon, projectile and charge had to be loaded separately, which slowed a rate of fire already adversely affected by the screw breech mechanism. This problem was rectified in the IS-3.

Josef Stalin tanks were at the head of the advance to Berlin in 1945 and remained in production after the war, and the model stayed the most powerful tank in service in the world for well over a decade.

KV-1

Named after a marshal of the Soviet Union – Klementy Voroshilov – the KV heavy tank was the third of a trio of designs in 1938 for a replacement for the T-35. The KV-1 was designed to withstand armour-piercing rounds, but not at the expense of mobility. A prototype was complete in September 1939, with several pre-production models seeing service in the Russo-Finnish War in 1940.

The main features of the tank were a centrally mounted turret containing a 76.2mm gun and two machine guns, a driver's compartment at the front with a hull machine-gun position to the left of the driver, and a rear-mounted diesel engine. The wide tracks helped to reduce ground pressure, and the vehicle had good armour protection. During the production run improvements were made to the tank, such as the adding of additional armour, which were welded onto the glacis and driver's plates but bolted onto the hull and turret sides.

At the time of the German invasion of the Soviet Union, 500 of both types of KV tank were in service. Overall the KV-1 was a good tank, but was outclassed when the German Tiger appeared in 1942. It was therefore modified, with the driver repositioned to the centre of the hull front and no hull machine gunner. A new turret was added to mount the 85mm gun – this tank was the KV-85.

SPECIFICATIONS

KV-1

Designation: KV-1	**Secondary Armament:** 3 x 7.62mm
Type: Heavy Tank	**Engine:** V-2K V-12 diesel 600hp
Length: 6.68m (21.9ft)	**Range:** 150km (93.2 miles)
Width: 3.32m (10.89ft)	**Speed:** 35km/h (21.75mph)
Height: 2.71m (8.75ft)	**Fording:** Unknown
Weight: 43,000kg (94,600lb)	**Trench Crossing:** Unknown
Crew: Five	**Armour (hull):** 30mm (1.18in)
Main Armament: 76.2mm	**Armour (turret):** 120mm (4.72in)

KV-2

SPECIFICATIONS

KV-2

Designation:
KV-2

Type:
Heavy Assault Tank

Length:
6.79m (22.3ft)

Width:
3.32m (10.89ft)

Height:
3.65m (12ft)

Weight:
53,963kg (118,720lb)

Crew:
Six

Main Armament:
152mm

Secondary Armament:
2 x 7.62mm

Engine:
V-2K V-12 diesel 600hp

Range:
140km (87.5 miles)

Speed:
25.6km/h (16mph)

Fording:
Unknown

Trench Crossing:
2.59m (8.5ft)

Armour (hull):
30mm (1.18in)

Armour (turret):
110mm (4.33in)

The KV-2 first appeared in early 1940, a massive and unwieldy vehicle that was an "artillery tank" version of the KV-1. It mounted a 152mm-calibre howitzer in a high, square turret that replaced the KV-1's turret. The turret itself had a 360-degree traverse, but it was heavy and the bearings were badly designed. This meant that the turret could only be fully traversed when the vehicle was on level ground. In addition, the increase in top-heavy weight with no corresponding increase in power meant decreased overall mobility. Ironically this meant little, for the gun could not be fired when the vehicle was on the move.

The KV-2 had the same chassis as the KV-1, and later versions had the wider tracks of the KV-1B as well as a slightly different turret and gun mounting. The KV-2 had some success against the Mannerheim Line defences during the war against Finland in 1940, but they were found to be totally useless against the fast-moving panzers during the German invasion of the Soviet Union in 1941.

Such were their inadequacies that they were not used after 1941, though since the chassis was identical to that used in the KV-1, it would seen likely that most surviving KV-2s were converted to KV-1s, which were sorely needed to combat the invading panzers.

T-26

A Soviet-built version of the British Vickers-Armstrong 6-ton Tank, the original T-26s were manufactured in both twin-turret and single-turret versions. However, from 1933 onwards production was concentrated on the single-turret model, in which a larger gun could be mounted. Production continued until 1939, the final variant being the T-26S, which differed externally from earlier models in the increased use of welded armour, with sloping hull plates and a more streamlined turret.

The air-cooled engine was positioned in the rear, the transmission being led forward to front-drive sprockets. Suspension consisted of two groups of four bogie wheels each side, sprung on quarter-elliptic leaf springs. The T-26B mounted the long 45mm high-velocity gun, with a coaxial machine gun and sometimes a second machine gun in the turret rear. Variants of this tank included a flamethrower version with the left turret removed and a flame gun fitted in the right turret, and a command tank equipped with a radio in the turret rear and a frame aerial round the turret.

The T-26 was an important factor in the tank strength of the Soviet Union during the 1930s, and was used against the Finns and the Germans in 1941. However, by this time it was obsolete and was therefore soon after phased out of service.

SPECIFICATIONS

T-26

Designation: **T-26**	Secondary Armament: **2 x 7.62mm**
Type: **Light Tank**	Engine: **Armstrong Siddeley 75hp**
Length: **4.8m (15.75ft)**	Range: **225km (140.6 miles)**
Width: **2.44m (8ft)**	Speed: **35.2km/h (22mph)**
Height: **2.05m (6.75ft)**	Fording: **Unknown**
Weight: **8654kg (19,040lb)**	Trench Crossing: **2.2m (7.21f)**
Crew: **Three**	Armour (hull): **6mm (.23in)**
Main Armament: **37mm**	Armour (turret): **13mm (.51in)**

T-33

SPECIFICATIONS

T-33

Designation:
T-33

Type:
Amphibious Tank

Length:
3.73m (12.23ft)

Width:
1.94m (6.26ft)

Height:
1.84m (6.03ft)

Weight:
3250kg (7150lb)

Crew:
Two

Main Armament:
1 x 7.62mm

Secondary Armament:
None

Engine:
GAZ-AA 70hp

Range:
185km (115.6 miles)

Speed:
35km/h (21.82mph)

Fording:
Amphibious

Trench Crossing:
Unknown

Armour (hull):
4mm (.15in)

Armour (turret):
9mm (.35in)

In 1931, the eight amphibious Carden-Loyd tankettes which had been purchased in England under the 1931 negotiations were used as the basis for a new light amphibious tank. This first prototype of the T-33 had a two-man crew. Armed with a single 7.62mm machine gun in a 360-degree traverse turret, its petrol engine provided 63hp. A second prototype of the T-33 was fitted with an improved suspension and a new armour arrangement.

The new suspension was a modified Horstmann scissors-type more suitable for Russian terrain. The second prototype was completed in 1933, and was designated T-37. The hull configuration was almost identical to that on the original Carden-Loyd tankette. New features included the turret fitted to the left, and modified tracks and propeller drive systems. The exterior of the vehicle was also strengthened against wave buffeting. The early production models, believed to have been designated 3-2T, had small welded turrets with flush tops, similar to those fitted on the T-26A.

The vehicle had a single propeller and rudder fitted on the rear hull, with a power takeoff from the engine for the propeller. Encased in sheet metal, balsa-wood floats were fitted in form of trackguards to provide additional buoyancy to the watertight hull.

T-35

The idea behind having a vehicle equipped with multiple turrets was the provision of all-round fire, combined with mobility. Thus the T-32, so built, was put into service in 1931, to be followed by the five-turret T-35 in 1933. The latter, which had a more powerful engine, increased ammunition stowage, reduced side skirts, thicker armour and the provision of a radio, continued in production until 1939, though only a maximum of 30 were built. They were massive vehicles, and were useful for propaganda purposes.

Each tank had a large turret mounting the main armament and four subsidiary turrets grouped round it. Main armament was the 76.2mm gun, with one machine gun in a ball mounting in the turret rear, while two of the auxiliary turrets (the front right and rear left) were armed with 45mm guns; the other two small turrets had one machine gun each. Early models were armed with 37mm guns, and other modifications involved the removal of the two machine-gun turrets.

The combat performance of the mighty T-35 was very poor. Always mechanically unreliable, they were deployed by the Red Army in 1941 to repel the German invasion, but most were captured when they either broke down or ran out of fuel before they reached the combat zone. Very few saw any actual fighting.

SPECIFICATIONS

T-35

Designation:
T-35

Type:
Heavy Tank

Length:
9.6m (31.5ft)

Width:
3.2m (10.49ft)

Height:
3.42m (11.25ft)

Weight:
45,818kg (100,800lb)

Crew:
10

Main Armament:
76.2mm

Secondary Armament:
2 x 45mm, 6 x 7.62mm

Engine:
M-17M, 500hp

Range:
150km (93.75 miles)

Speed:
30km/h (18.75mph)

Fording:
Unknown

Trench Crossing:
2.29m (7.51ft)

Armour (hull):
11mm (.43in)

Armour (turret):
52mm (.98in)

T-34/76

SPECIFICATIONS

T-34/76

Designation:
T-34/76

Type:
Medium Tank

Length:
6.58m (21.6ft)

Width:
3m (9.84ft)

Height:
2.43m (8ft)

Weight:
26,778kg (58,912lb)

Crew:
Four

Main Armament:
76.2mm

Secondary Armament:
2 x 7.62mm

Engine:
V-2-34 V-12 500hp

Range:
186km (115 miles)

Speed:
50km/h (31mph)

Fording:
1.37m (4.5ft)

Trench Crossing:
2.95m (9.66ft)

Armour (hull):
20mm (.78in)

Armour (turret):
52mm (2.04in)

One of the most decisive weapons of World War II, the T-34 was developed from the BT series of tanks. The first prototypes were produced in early 1940, and after some modifications the first production models rolled out of the Kirov Tank Plant in June 1940. By the time the Germans invaded the Soviet Union in 1941, over 1200 had been built.

The design of the T-34 was excellent, and made effective use of sloped armour plates for the hull. This, combined with the 76.2mm gun and 500hp diesel engine, had a profound effect on the Germans when they encountered them in battle. Ironically, few features of the T-34 were original, having appeared in one form or another in earlier Soviet or foreign tanks. The basic layout placed the engine at the rear, with a Christie-type suspension, and large road wheels on pivot arms controlled by long coil springs. The tracks were held together by pins that were retained in place only by plates attached to the hull, which pushed back the heads of any projecting pins as they passed – this made for simple track maintenance.

The driver sat at the front, beside the co-driver who operated a machine gun mounted in the glacis plate. The 76.2mm gun shared a mounting with a 7.62mm machine gun.

T-34/85

In response to the German Panzer IV armed with the long-barrelled 75mm gun and the Tiger with the 88mm gun, the Soviets increased the T-34's hull frontal armour to 100mm (3.93in) and up-gunned it with the long-barrelled 85mm L51.5 gun. This was an excellent weapon, capable of taking on German Panthers and Tigers on an equal footing. A tank version of the Soviet 85mm antiaircraft gun, it was also used as the armament for the SU-85 tank destroyer. To accommodate the weapon the turret was enlarged, being modified from that developed from the KV-85.

The T-34/85 entered service in early 1944 and was an excellent fighting vehicle. That said, by 1943 it was being outclassed by the German Tiger plus the numerous 88mm-armed antitank vehicles in enemy service, notably the Elefant and Hornisse. It was decided, therefore, to design an even more powerfully armed replacement – the T-44. However, it was beset with problems and the T-34/85 soldiered on.

Between 1940 and 1945, some 40,000 T-34 tanks of all models were produced, and manufacture continued after the war. By the early 1960s, for example, this figure had reached nearly 55,000 vehicles. Though it was never as good as the Tiger and Panther on a one-to-one basis, the sheer numbers produced made the T-34 a war winner.

SPECIFICATIONS

T-34/85

Designation:
T-34/85

Type:
Medium Tank

Length:
7.49m (24.6ft)

Width:
2.93m (9.61ft)

Height:
2.37m (7.8ft)

Weight:
32,073kg (70,560lb)

Crew:
Five

Main Armament:
85mm

Secondary Armament:
1 x 7.62mm

Engine:
140km (87.5 miles)

Range:
310km (193.75 miles)

Speed:
55km/h (34.37mph)

Fording:
1.3m (4.26ft)

Trench Crossing:
2.95m (9.66ft)

Armour (hull):
100mm (3.93in)

Armour (turret):
90mm (3.54in)

INDEX